STREET LIFE

POVERTY, GANGS, AND A Ph.D.

First Edition

DR. VICTOR RIOS

Five Rivers Press,
California

D0048856

For Multiple Book Orders or Speaking Engagements Please Contact:

streetlife@fiveriverspress.com
     Or

drvictorrios@mac.com

For individual orders please visit:

https://www.createspace.com/3485381

or Amazon.com

CONTENTS

Preface

I write this book knowing that young people who face adversity have the power to transform their lives, turn their struggles into their strengths, and accomplish the unbelievable. In order to generate the spark that will ignite this process of transformation among young people placed at risk, educators, parents, community members, and politicians must do their part. We have to begin by eradicating the idea that those young people who have shown signs of delinquency, bullying, gang affiliation, or defiance are irreparable and "unteachable." And, for those young people who have given up on themselves, who have lost hope, who live what we perceive as fatalistic lives, we have to believe in them so much that we trick them into believing in themselves.

This book is written to speak to a young adult audience—those young people who live on the margins, who are often assigned texts that do not represent their lived reality, their struggles, or their experiences. Educators and youth workers can use each of the short chapters in this book as tools for discussing complicated social issues like abuse, youth violence, delinquency, fatalism, opportunity, stratification, poverty, resilience, college, positive role models, healthy choices, and personal transformation.

My goal is that by reading about my journey through detrimental conditions—some created by others and some created by myself—students will become inspired to take charge of their choices and lives, and adults will compliment this process by opening more doors of opportunity to these at-promise young people.

I also write this book to compliment my other 2011 book, *Punished: Policing the Lives of Black and Latino Boys*, published by New York University Press. In that book, I talk about the many ways in which marginalized young people are abandoned and punished by school, law enforcement, and the community, and how this leads to delinquency and a lack of educational attainment. Readers who wish to read a more in-depth narrative and theoretical formulation about some of the issues discussed in this book may want to acquire a copy of *Punished*. Read together, these two books provide insight to agency and structure, the personal and the systematic, the individual and the historical, the psychological and the sociological. Any one of these cannot be understood without the other.

I look forward to amazing discussions with young people and adults about the stories that follow. It is in these discussions that I hope we can come together to provide young people the tools for overcoming the many adversities that they encounter in our society.

1

Standing Ovation

I am the rose that grew from concrete.
 –Tupac Shakur

I sit on a stage at the Los Angeles Convention Center, surrounded by an ocean of 5,000 people staring at me. I grip my nervous right leg to stop it from uncontrollably shaking. The master of ceremonies starts to introduce me. Even though her voice transmits through a dozen giant speakers, I cannot make sense of the words she speaks. I am too focused on collecting my thoughts and trying to make my stomach quiet down from all the grumbling sounds it's making; my intestines feel like a high performance car at a sideshow, spinning 360 degrees, full circle. I am supposed to be preparing myself to inspire these parents, students, and teachers for 45 minutes. I have been invited here, to the Los Angeles School District's Parent Summit, to tell my story of struggle with poverty, gangs, violence, and juvenile hall, and to provide tools for helping other young people who face similar obstacles. I stand up, walk to the podium, and shake the master of ceremonies' hand. A giant spotlight beams right into my eyes, halfway blinding me, but the glare of this light is not going to stop me from telling my story. In the past, I have faced bigger, deadlier challenges.

1

I collect my thoughts, grip on to the podium for confidence, take a deep breath, look at the audience, and begin to speak.

As I finish my talk, the crowd begins to clap. I see a middle-aged, grey-haired teacher stand up. She continues clapping, and then two other people, a mother and her teenage son, stand up and continue clapping. Entire rows of people begin to stand. Suddenly, like fans celebrating a home run at an L.A. Dodgers game, the entire audience is on their feet! A standing ovation!

Dozens of people line up to get my autograph and take a picture with me. One student, a 15-year-old homeboy wearing baggy Dickies pants, white Nike Air Force One tennis shoes, and an extra long white t-shirt, approaches me and says, "Dr. Rios, you just told my story." A mother, her eyes full of tears, taps me on the shoulder and says, "You are my son, I mean, you are just like my son. God bless you." Then, the teacher who stood up from her seat to spark the standing ovation walks up to me. She tells me that she has many students like me, and that I have reignited her fire to motivate young people placed at risk to persist, survive, and transform.

Who would have thought that this homey from the "ghetto," who was often seen as a "good-for-nothing-drug-slanging-gang-banging-Mexican-criminal," would be here, on this stage, today?

I am an award winning sociology professor at the University of California, Santa Barbara. I have a doctorate degree from the University of California, Berkeley. But I'm supposed to be locked up in a six-foot by nine-foot prison cell at San Quentin State

2

Penitentiary, doing twenty-five-years to life alongside my homeboy Rambo. He stabbed someone to death, in front of me, when we were 15-years-old. I am supposed to be out on the streets of Oakland, California, shooting up heroine or snorting meth with some of the guys I grew up with, who are stealing and robbing to get high, as I write this. Instead, I have written two books.

Many of my homies did not make it because they encountered many obstacles growing up. Poverty, violence, drug abuse, parental and school neglect, and criminalization carved out many of their paths. If they had encountered some of the opportunities I discovered, maybe they would also have acquired success. In this world, it takes hard work and opportunity to make it. A person has to be ready to change, in order to make it to the next level, but opportunities have to be provided, as well.

From an early age, I was not ready to change; I was fatalistic. I did not believe in myself, and thought I would not make it to my 18th birthday. "I am not supposed to be here," I told myself, "School isn't for me! SCHOOL IS NOT FOR ME!" I would say to myself, "Why do I want to go to school, if it is not paying me money to help my mom with the bills?" "Why do I want to go to school, if every time I am there, the teachers and principal treat me like I don't belong?" "Why do I want to go to school, if every time I am there, I get in a fight with guys who try to bully me?" I lost faith in myself early on. Losing faith, feeling inferior, being neglected, and fleeing poverty and tragedy led me on a path of self-destruction. This book discusses my journey through an atrocious upbringing, and shows the steps that I took to take control of the obstacles I encountered.

I have always believed that the best way to connect with people is to open up, to tell my story and expose my past, even if this means showing some weakness. This process has allowed me to gain trust in others, and, in response, many young people have shared their stories. In this book, I would like to invite the reader to walk a mile in my shoes: to examine the obstacles that I had to face growing up; to explore how I managed to transform my life and overcome adversity; and, to find solutions, so that one day soon, many more young people, who face similar circumstances, can stand on a stage and tell their stories of success. Instead of being treated like criminals and being neglected, these young people could feel the support of their teachers, parents, and community giving them a standing ovation. My hope is that the story I tell inspires others to continue cultivating the seeds that will flourish to end youth violence, improve our schools, and make our communities safer places to live.

2

In Jail Before Birth

Some people are always whining
because roses have thorns, I am
thankful that thorns have roses.
-Alphonse Karr

My mother Raquel was a tough woman. At age 15,
she found herself, alone, on the poor streets of
Mexico City, with not a cent to her name. She had to
protect herself from predators who tried to abuse
her. She learned to fight, and to show no emotions
even in the most traumatic moments. When she was
13, she was kidnapped by a man and taken as his
wife. He beat and abused her. A few months later,
her cousin, also 13 years old, came to find her. He
confronted her abuser, and, in front of my mother,
hit him in the head with a steel rebar. The guy fell
on the ground; my mother's cousin grabbed the
man's pistol and unloaded the entire clip into him.

From that time on, my mother became numb to her
experiences in life. She lived life showing no
emotion, and was ready to take on any fight that
came her way. My mother Raquel never allowed any
man to disrespect her. If one of her boyfriends tried
to hit her, she would hit him back. If a guy tried to
tell her what to do, she would talk back or end the
relationship altogether.

6

My mother's strengths also became her weaknesses. Shutting her emotions off from the world led her to treat my siblings and me with very little affection. She provided food and shelter, when she could, and expected us to go to school, but she rarely hugged us or told us she loved us. This marked me with pain, seeking a mother's love when all that she could do was to teach us how to be tough in life.

My mother's painful experiences led to a debilitating depression. Unfortunately, she was not diagnosed until her children were adults. She often took her pain out on me, telling me that she wished she had succeeded in her attempts to abort me. At seven-years-old, a tiny little boy, with jet-black hair and a good sense of humor, I would run under my apartment stairs and cry for hours, thinking that I was not wanted in this world. My mother eventually gave me details on her attempt to abort me.

When she was six months pregnant, with me in her belly, Raquel got into a fight with a woman at a bar. In the middle of the fight, Raquel threw a chair at her rival. As the chair sailed through the air, the tip of one of its sharp legs sliced right through the woman's face. The woman was sent to the hospital; my mother was sent to jail.

In jail, Raquel tried to abort me. She decided that she was too poor and too young to take care of a second child. She could hardly care for my older brother, J.T., aged four. Abortion was illegal in Mexico, so she decided to try it on her own. She carried 5 gallon buckets full of water, one in each arm, back and forth through the prison. She began to feel her uterus trying to expel me, with pain and blood spouting. Other prisoners noticed my mother's unhealthy practice of attempting to abort me. They stopped her from carrying the heavy buckets. One of the women told her that she was not going to allow my mother to get rid of her baby nor kill herself. She grabbed my mother by the waist, and with other prisoners, pinned her down. These women, together, were stronger than Raquel. They watched my mother until a doctor arrived. He gave her a few shots of medication. A few months later, my mother was released from jail, and, a few days after that, I was born.

Raquel had a rough childhood which led her to sometimes neglect and abandon her own children. I don't blame her for the all the harm that she caused my siblings and I. In the end, she provided us with shelter, food, and an expectation to find a better life for ourselves. I give thanks that my mother was convinced to give birth to me. I realize that some people are not meant to be parents and that they don't know how to properly nurture their children. Having been raised by a mother that had some of these issues I had to learn early on to nurture myself, to promise myself that when I was older and had children I would make sure to show them love, affection, and appreciation.

My mother should have had the right to choose what was best for her body. If she had had adequate healthcare and lived in a country where abortion was not illegal, maybe she would have made the right choice for herself during the first few months of her pregnancy.

But in jail, she was over six months pregnant, a little too late to turn back the clock. By then, I believe, it was my destiny to be born.

3

The Bastard

Adversity causes some to break; others to break records.
-William Ward

I grew up never meeting my father. Every day of my life I searched for him, and, finally, 31 years later, I found him. I only knew two things about my father, his name and that he was once in the Mexican military. I wanted to find him to learn more about his side of the family, so that, one day, if my kids ever asked me about their grandfather and his family, I could come up with an answer for them. I was also curious to know what my father looked like and how similar we were to each other.

I called a cousin of mine in Mexico and asked her to help me gather some records from the military. She called me back a few weeks later; she had located my father's address. Soon after that, I was on a plane to Mexico. It was a long trip from California to Michoacan, Mexico, the city near where my father lived. I picked up a rental car there, and drove for a few hours looking for the town he lived in, Las Guacamayas. The drive was majestic: lush, green, rainforest vegetation surrounded the highway on each side; the pacific ocean beat its waves against the land; and spectacular, huge yellow butterflies zipped past me as I drove.

Finding Las Guacamayas, I began to search for my father's home. As I got close to his house, I noticed little kids splashing in a canal that made its way to the ocean. Finally, when I got to his house, I took a deep breath, walked to his door, planted my feet firmly on the ground to keep my right leg from shaking with fear, and knocked. A fifty-year-old man, with dark brown skin, the color of mine, and his nose the mirror image of mine, answered the door.

I asked him, "Is your name Cecilio Nava?"

"Yes," he said. I introduced myself. He looked at me and nodded. "Good, he said, "What do you need from me?"

It was a good question, and I hesitated while I thought how to answer. Finally, I realized that he thought I was there to ask him for money. I told him, "I don't need anything from you; I just wanted to meet you." We shook hands; I asked him a few questions: "Where are you from? Who are your parents? Where do they live? Do you have more children?" He answered with brief responses.

After I ran out of questions, there was a moment of awkward silence. I had the kind of feeling one gets when first meeting a complete stranger and having nothing in common with him. He told me he had to go. I told him I also had to go, even though I would have liked to get to know him. It seemed he was shocked by the experience of meeting me, and, also, that I had let my pride get the best of me. We shook hands again.

I got into my rental car, drove to the airport, and headed home to my family in California. After I returned, I realized that I had forgotten to ask my father a very important question, "Why did you abandon me?"

When my mother was three months pregnant with me, she took a trip to visit her parents. When she came back, my father was gone with no explanation. After I was born, she gave me her last name. My mother believed that my father did not deserve to have a child with his last name, if he was not around to raise him.

The older I became, the more I yearned to know my father, and the more ashamed I felt for not having one. I was ten when one of my classmates asked me, "How come your father never comes to school?"

"I don't have a father," I told him.

He laughed, louder and louder, until everyone was looking, and then yelled out: "Victor is a bastard!"

During recess, I walked up behind this classmate, and, before he got a chance to make a complete turn, I punched him in the face. We scuffled for a few minutes, until the yard duty separated us and took us to the office. But it was too late. My nickname for the school year became "bastard."

I was called bastard hundreds of times that year. Every time I walked into class, I heard, "There goes the bastard." Every time I walked past the rusty school fence on my way home from school, I heard, "bastard, bastard, bastard." While I did not know the exact meaning of the word, it cut deeply. What was worse was that being called that name reminded me that growing up without a father made me an incomplete person; I felt less than human. I felt like a dog at the pound. Each time someone called me bastard, my chest shriveled, and my eyes would tear up in anger and pain.

Growing up fatherless was very painful. Today, however, I think about the benefits of growing up without a father. Many of my friends had fathers who neglected them, beat them, and never played a game of soccer with them. What if I had a father who was an asshole to my mother and me? Maybe not having a father was not so bad after all. Growing up fatherless allowed me to seek out father figures that I wanted to have, like my Uncle Tito, who taught me how to work on cars; my brother J.T, who, despite being so young, always cared for me and guided me; or my neighbor Carnell, who showed me how to throw a real punch, "Use your hip, son," he would tell me.

Not having a father forced me to promise myself that if I ever had children, I would do everything in my power to be a good role model, to be there for them, to provide for them, and to never abandon them.

Not having a father gave me the strength to always seek out guidance from surrogate parents, people whom I could rely on to support me in my struggles.

4

Homeless and Hungry

Poverty is the worst form of violence.
-Mahatma Ghandi

My older brother Juan, whom we call "J.T.," was
ecstatic when I was born. He was just four-years-old,
and had wanted a baby brother ever since he was
two. J.T wanted a younger brother, and when my
mother told him she was pregnant, he was thrilled.
But when I came home, he was sorry he had wished
for me. All I did was cry. He said I sounded like
someone was torturing me and that I would not shut
up. My mother told me that J.T. complained, and
told her, "I asked for a baby brother but not a cry
baby brother."

There was a reason why I cried. I had parasites,
worms that lived in my baby intestines. I was
hospitalized twice by the time I was a toddler for my
stomach illness. My mother says I almost died. We
don't know how I got the parasites, but my mother
was so poor she often fed me old milk. We didn't have
a refrigerator; neither did the many relatives we
stayed with when we had no place to go. The milk
would sit out at room temperature during the warm
Mexican nights, growing bacteria. The rotten milk
made me more ill. My stomach grumbled in the

middle of the night, sharp pains attacked me. I cried all night.

We were homeless, living in one of the biggest cities in the world, Mexico City, moving from one relative's home to another. The relatives we stayed with were also poor, and the living conditions were dire. We often slept in small, crowded, concrete shacks with tin roofs and dirt floors. My mother became desperate. She continued to look for a way out of our suffering. She yearned for a better place, where her children could have a better future, and where her hard work could at least pay for a decent shelter and a few meals a day for her family.

One day, when we were staying with my mother's aunt, Rosa, she told my mother to solve her problems by taking her children north, to the land of opportunity, a place where nobody goes hungry, where everyone is happy, where money grows on trees, and where everyone has a house with a swimming pool!

I don't know what kind of movies my Aunt Rosa was watching, or what she was smoking, but my mother believed her. My mother began to prepare for the journey. She saved every peso she could earn to get us on a bus to the US-Mexico Border and to pay for the crossing. She told relatives about her big journey and about her fears of getting lost, losing her children, being robbed, raped, incarcerated, or killed on the heartless border. But she also thought about the endless world of possibilities that might come after crossing the border. She created an illusion for herself. My mother thought that the minute she crossed the border into the United States of America she would have a good job, my stomach parasites would disappear, we would not go hungry, and maybe she could even become rich.

We took a long two-day bus ride from Mexico City to Tijuana, the place where dreams go to die. Our hopes shrank as soon as we talked with U.S. Immigration agents at the U.S. border. They told us that we were poor and uneducated, and that we had no chance of entering the U.S.

Like millions of other Mexican migrants running away from pain and suffering and hurdling towards a life of opportunity, my mother decided to cross the border illegally. She found a Coyote, a human smuggler, who helped people get across. In exchange for information, she paid him the final stash of money she had, which she had kept hidden in the lining of her bra.

We met the Coyote at a bus stop and took a bus to a remote area near a giant border fence. Walking towards the fence, we found a hole in the bottom; we crawled under the fence and came up on the U.S. side. My mother grabbed my 7-year-old brother by the hand, and threw me, 3-years-old, onto her hip. We walked through a desert stream in the dry heat of the dessert. Soon after, two towering U.S. Border Patrol vans, with 4x4 tires as tall as my older brother, drove up to us. The Coyote told my mother to run as he made his own escape. He got away, but my mother stuck around with us, knowing that we could not get far. Border Patrol officers approached my mother and muscled her into a van. They told her that she would never see us again, and drove off. I remember going into shock, dropping onto the dusty desert soil and screaming and crying for my mother. My brother walked up to me, grabbed my arm, and yanked me up from the ground. The Border Patrol officers grabbed my brother and me, and put us into the back of a separate van. The van had metal bench seats and two small caged windows, hiding us in this dark mobile prison from the bright dessert sun.

My brother and I clutched each other's hand tightly, and began to cry. One Border Patrol agent noticed us crying and began to laugh. He told us that my mother was going to jail forever. We believed him. I was three years old and J.T. was only seven years old, but to me he was the most responsible adult I knew. J.T. told me not to worry, that he would take care of me now, and I believed him.

The agents lied. A few hours after they separated us, they brought us to my mother. We ran to her, leaping into her arms. We were so excited to see her we did not think what it meant when the agents released us onto the streets of Tijuana. We would end up homeless and hungry; the streets were unforgiving. Cars and buses crowded the streets, honking and filling the air with black smoke; hundreds of people walked the streets, pushing even the smallest of kids aside when they got in their way; many poor mothers with their own hungry children loitered on the sidewalks. Like other families on the busy streets of Tijuana, we lived by begging. I remember having to stick my hand out, begging people for money so that we could eat. I remember seeing my mother stick her hand out and beg for money. She would say: "Por favor, un pecito para alimentar a mis hijos." ["Please, can you spare one penny to feed my children."]

My mother had to make a choice: starve or wither away on the streets of Tijuana, or risk our lives and freedom and try to cross the border again. She chose to cross. She called a friend who lived in the United States, and she also called J.T.'s father, to ask them both for a loan so that she could hire another Coyote. J.T.'s father, Marcos, spent some time in Tijuana with us, helping us prepare for the journey. While we lived in Tijuana he rented us a hotel room, worked as a mechanic, and took care of us while my mother disappeared looking for ways to fund our trip across the border.

Eventually, Marcos and other family members loaned her the money to pay for the journey across. The Coyote told my mother that J.T. and I had to cross separately in order to have a better chance of making it. The Coyote took the two of us through some hills, across the desert, and behind many bushes. Finally, after hours of waiting we made it across the border. But we did not know if our mother had made it across.

The Coyotes got us across, but they lost the address my mother had given them. At a loss for what to do with two young children, they kept us locked in a room of a house full of people for a week. They barely fed us. They gave us cold, uncooked tortillas with salt, and, if we were lucky, they would bring us cereal and milk. My brother heard them say that they would drop us off in front of the Mexican consulate if my mother did not contact them.

J.T. fed me, bathed me, and comforted me, as I cried for our mother. He remembers me playing with a small toy car. On one of the days we spent in the locked room, my toy car fell through the cracks of the broken wood floor. I cried tirelessly for my comfort toy. My brother did everything he could to get it, and, after a few hours of trying to grab the toy with a pencil he found, he got my car back for me. J.T. was my hero and he continued to inspire me and support me as we grew up.

Ten days later, my mother tracked us down in Los Angeles. She promised us we would never be separated again. Then she told us to get ready. It was time to look for work in the land of opportunity. We had made it to "los Estados Unidos," the United States of America, the land where dreams come true. Or, so we thought.

5

Land of the Rats

What makes the desert beautiful
is that somewhere it hides a well.
-Antoine de Saint-Exupery

We spent a few weeks in Los Angeles, where my mother worked as a house cleaner. After saving up enough money for three Greyhound Bus tickets, we made the move to Oakland, California. A woman my mother befriended in Tijuana, Angelica, who made the journey across before us, invited her to Oakland. Angelica related to my mother. They both had rough upbringings, and they both liked to drink and go to bars. My mother contacted Angelica when we stayed in L.A. According to my mom, Angelica told her, "You have to come to Oakland. It is beautiful here. There is a big tower here with a big clock on it, and anywhere you are in the downtown area, you know what time it is. The streets are paved with cement here instead of dirt! And guess what? People here ride around in buses instead of on burros!"

The glamour of a new land, a new adventure, new opportunities, and a new drinking buddy, attracted my mother to Oakland. The bus ride there seemed like another eternity. We sat in the back of the bus, close to the bathroom. A man, who reeked of liquor, walked towards the bathroom, stumbling and falling right next to where I sat. He looked at me, smiled and threw up. The disgusting vomit, along with the worst smell I can remember ever smelling, made my sensitive stomach react. I also began throwing up, over my only pair of pants, and on my mother's arm.

Upon finally arriving in Oakland, we moved in with my mother's friend, Angelica. She lived in a tiny studio with no private bathroom. The apartment complex had common toilets and showers, like a workout facility, where anyone could enter while you showered, at any time.

Finding work was not easy for my mother. She spoke not one word of English, had a third grade education, and had very little work experience. The job my mother finally got was more servitude than employment. The minimum wage in the U.S. at the time was $3.10 an hour. Her boss, the owner of the restaurant where she cleaned tables and swept the floor, paid her $2.00 an hour. My mother tried to complain to her boss about the low pay; he responded by threatening her. He told her that he would call immigration enforcement officers if she complained so that they could deport her.

While my mother slaved away at her low paying job, my brother and I waited in the crowded studio apartment nine hours a day. My mother did not have a childcare provider for us, so she would leave for work with us locked in the studio. My brother, a 7-year-old child, was in charge of taking care of me, a 3-year-old child, while we were locked in that room for nine hours. I don't know how he managed to keep us both safe, but he did a great job. He was the only trustworthy person I knew, so I leaned on him for support and when I needed a shoulder to cry on. J.T. remembers that we used to try to make an old black-and-white television work so that we could watch cartoons. He says that we were lucky if we were able to watch a show for 20 minutes before the television turned into a noisy grey and black dotted screen. I remember watching M.A.S.H. with him, a show about Army doctors who lived in the jungle in South Korea.

A few months later, my mother was able to enroll my brother in school and find a daycare center for me. It took her a few months to get us enrolled in school because we had to get immunized and establish proof of residency. She also saved a modest amount of money to rent our own place. We lived on International Avenue, near 21st Street. We moved several times, and each condemned apartment seemed to be getting worse.

At one point, we ended up living in the "Lower Bottom" of West Oakland. We rented a one bedroom apartment in an old Victorian house with nothing victorious about it. Roaches would creep into our cereal boxes and have tiny babies that we found floating in the milk of our morning cereal. Killing one roach seemed to make more appear, crawling out from behind the refrigerator, under our cabinets, and behind our walls. My skin still gets goose bumps when I remember when the roaches crawled on me, tickling the hair on my arms, in the middle of the night.

When crack addicts broke our window to steal from us, the landlord put up a giant piece of plywood, instead of a new window. Our home seemed more like a cave than an apartment, and, to make matters worse, my mother sometimes couldn't afford to pay the electric bill. She would send us to beg the neighbors to let us run an orange extension cord from their apartment to ours, so that we could plug in a light bulb. Even when we had gas, the water heater was broken, and we didn't have warm water for baths. In order to take a warm bath, we had to boil water. My mother would turn on all the burners on the stove in a futile attempt to keep us warm at night. I remember smelling bad fumes all night long while I shivered under my thin blanket.

Giant Norwegian rats gnawed on our walls and ran across our peeled off linoleum floor, sounding like miniature tap dancing people. The rats were the size of small cats, with long tails the size of small garden snakes. One day, as I lay in the closet space under the neighbor's staircase, where my mother had placed an old mattress for me to sleep on, I heard a loud scratching noise on the ceiling. When I looked up, a few crumbs of sheetrock fell into my eye. Something was trying to break through the ceiling, right above me. I threw the old dingy sheet I used as a blanket over my head, and then, I felt them. Two giant rats had gnawed through the ceiling and leaped unto my bed. They ran around in circles on my bed as if they were happy about scaring the piss out of me. I froze, then unstuck, and kicked my legs as far as I could. The rats flew into the kitchen, running their happy circles on the kitchen floor.

I remember praying not to be cold at night; not to have to walk to school on an empty stomach; not to witness any more shootings and stabbings on the streets; and not to see my mother cry every night because she could not afford to pay the bills. My prayers went unanswered for many years.

Sometimes, I even questioned if god existed, since he never seemed to bring miracles to my neighborhood. As I grew older, instead of seeing improvements, I saw regressions; I felt more pain, and I grew desperate to escape the pain. My desperation to run away from poverty became more and more extreme.

When I started middle school, my baby cousin was attacked by rats. My aunt, uncle, and cousins lived next door. They had just arrived from Mexico, one of many families who followed my pioneering mother to Oakland, after she had taken the first brave step to settle in this lonely place. One day, as my three-month-old cousin slept in the apartment next door in his crib, the rats came. They crawled into his crib in the middle of the night. As his mother slept, the rats attacked him, chewing on his cheeks, lips, and gums. By the time his mother woke up and turned on the light, those rats had nearly chewed his face off. Ricky was in the hospital for three months so that doctors could put his face back together. At this point, I told myself, "I don't want to live like this; I don't want to be poor; I don't want my family to suffer."

My mother eventually remarried, and had two more children, my little sister, Rosa, and my little brother,

Mike. She got together with a cowboy-boot-wearing, hard-working, Mexican guy by the name of Juan Diaz. He worked as a cook at a Charley Brown's Steakhouse. Juan was a decent man. He would take the family to the flea market on Saturdays and to church, out for donuts, and to the park on Sundays. He was a hard disciplinarian. If you got out of line, he would pull out his own, huge, cowboy belt and whip us with it, or worse, he would kick us with his pointy "paisa" cowboy boots. Juan's income helped the family become more financially stable. However, this stability did not last for too long. Juan and my mother ran into problems and separated a few times. Eventually they divorced, and things got worse again. We ended up living in the same conditions we lived in before my mother met Juan.

6

Dropping Out

Only the educated are free
-Epictitus

At the age of thirteen, after reflecting on the rat attack on my cousin and on my mother's divorce, and deciding that I did not want to live in poverty any longer, I decided to drop out of school and look for work. While deep inside I knew that to stay in school was the right thing for me to do, I also had lost faith in school. I remember not liking school, starting in the third grade, when my teacher, Ms. Jackson, sent me out of the classroom for not reading a word on the blackboard. I sat in the front of the class. She called my name and asked me to read the word on the board. I nodded my head and whispered, "I can't." Ms. Jackson told me that if I did not read the word, I would be sent to the office. I nodded my head again. She yelled at me, and sent me to the principal.

What my teacher did not know was that I could not see the word on the board. I needed glasses. We were so poor that my mother never had the time, or the money, to have my eyes checked. It was not my fault that I could not read the word on the board, and yet the teacher yelled at me, and sent me to the principal. From this point on, I began to shut down in the classroom, and most teachers did not seem to care that I did. It wasn't until 10th grade that I found a teacher who wanted to know why I had shut down at school. I did not get my first pair of glasses until I was 13 years old, and I did not start wearing my glasses regularly until 11th grade.

So, one day, instead of walking to school, I walked to the local gardener's house. His name was Juan Jose Maria Guadalupe de la Garza. I called him Johnny for short. I asked him for a job and he told me: "I can't give you a job, you're too little, go back to school, mocoso [brat]."

I begged: "Johnny, please man! Let me get a job, my momma's broke. Pay me whatever you want."

"Pay you whatever I want? O.K. Get in the car, let's go." I had gotten a job, and it felt good. My dream was simple. If I could only have what the rich people had, whose front yards I mowed and cleaned, I would be happy. My dream kept me working for Johnny.

One day, I was cutting the lawn at a beautiful three-story home with a swimming pool, located in the hills of Oakland. An old lady pulled up in a Mercedes Benz. She had curly white hair, and had a little dog on her lap who also had curly white hair. I looked at the dog, I looked at the Mercedes Benz, and I looked at the three-story home with the swimming pool. At this point I told myself "when I grow up I want this house, I want that Mercedes, and I want that dog with the curly white hair!"

I continued to push the lawnmower with my small hands, as if I was pushing myself towards these things. I pushed lawn mowers that weighed more than me; I cut shrubs and roses that inserted their razor-sharp thorns into my arms, leaving gashes that would later get infected and spit out white, creamy puss. I dug trenches deep into the ground with a shovel, bent over for hours. Johnny paid me $1.00 an hour when the minimum wage was $4.25 an hour.

When Johnny handed me my first ten-dollar bill, I wanted to punch him in the face. "If you don't like it you can go back to school, cabron [smut]," he said. I was living in an illusion telling myself that if I worked hard, beating my body up, like my uncles and mother, I would one day become rich.

At the time, I didn't realize that the people who owned the nice houses, and drove Mercedes, and owned little dogs with curly white hair, weren't gardeners. They were doctors, lawyers, engineers, and business people. They were people who worked with their minds. They were people who had gone to college and gotten an education. While my mother had taught me a hard work ethic, I did not realize that there were two types of hard work. Here I was thinking that to make it out of poverty I had to work my body when in reality I had to work my mind.

7

The

Snake Belt

De la astilla sale la rosa
(from the thorn comes the rose).
-Raquel Rios

I didn't go to school for three months, and my
mother didn't know because our phone was shut
off. The school couldn't reach her. One of my
mom's boyfriends, a recent immigrant from
Mexico, stayed in our apartment while my mom
was at work and we where at school. He called his
brothers, sisters, and parents in Mexico, and when
the $500 phone bill arrived, he told my mother
that maybe they should stop seeing each other. He
left, and we ended up with no phone.

The school sent my mom letters, but I checked the
mail, and threw them out.   Finally, my friend's
mother told my mom that I had dropped out of
school. I came home that day to my mother
standing at the front door, half of her face covered
by the shadow of the splintering wooden door.
"Donde has estado?" [Where have you been?] I
looked down at the layers of caked dirt on my
pants, and brushed at them nervously. Big flakes
of dried dirt, the size of Frosted Flakes cereal, fell

on my mother's freshly mopped floor, which still smelled of Pine Sol.

I told her I was playing marbles. "Don't lie to me!" she said. She pulled her hand out from behind her back, revealing a thick leather belt in her fist. There wasn't a man in our house, but my mother made sure that she had a man's belt. We called it "el cinturon de la vivora," the snake belt, because a big, printed snake curled across it, and left a big snake mark on our culos [bottoms]when she hit us with it.

Afraid of being beaten, I told my mother the truth; I had been working to help pay the bills. I reached into my pocket and pulled out a big stack of one-dollar bills, and tried to hand it to her. She hit me anyway, but before she did, she yelled at me.

"I don't want your money! I want you to go to school! I have worked too hard to get you to this country! I have worked too hard to get clothes on your back! I may not have money to give you, but I work hard to feed you and keep you alive! How can you leave school after all this hard work I have done? I didn't suffer all these years for you to become a dropout!" My mother may not have been perfect but she expected us to go to school to improve our livelihood.

Getting a whipping was painful. But worse, I had backstabbed my own mother, betrayed her hopes for me to finish school, after all of her pain and hard work. Even though my mother had made many mistakes while raising me, she had always made sure that we had a place to live and basic food, and she had a deep desire to see us finish school. I thought that the least I could do for my mother was to pay her back for having given birth to me. To make my mother proud, to thank her for keeping me alive and sheltered, I decided to go back to school.

8

A True
Gangster

The mother of revolution
and crime is poverty.
-Aristotle

I made an effort to return to school, in an attempt to
appease my mom. At least, I tried to go back to
school. But, at age thirteen, I felt like a man. My
body was changing. My bicep muscles had grown big
from pushing all those lawn mowers while I was
gardening; I wore a white, tank-top shirt to show off
my muscles. A few facial hairs started growing on
my chin. I would stare at the mirror and pull on
those few hairs to see if more hairs would grow; I
wanted to have a beard and a moustache. Also, my
body started doing all kinds of weird, uncontrollable
things. It was an awkward and embarrassing time
for me.

I also started dressing differently, wearing the
baggiest Ben Davis pants that I could find at the
Goodwill Thrift Store. With the money I saved while
I had a job, I bought myself a brand new pair of
white leather Nike Cortez shoes. I shaved my head,
and when my hair starting growing out, I greased it
up with Tres Flores hair pomade and wore a hair net.
I did all of this to try to impress the girls in the
neighborhood. I would slowly stroll by them, trying

to look cool. As I walked, I would look up towards the sky and my body would lean back like a cholo.

My uncle caught me walking like this one day and asked me: "Mi'jo, did you just crap your pants? Because you are walking around like you have a big piece of cagada hanging in your pants!" My uncle gave me a new nickname, "el cagado," the guy who crapped his pants.

Trying to look cool got me into trouble. One day, when I was walking home from school, a group of older boys, the guys who'd dropped out of school and were roaming the streets living the gang life, started walking towards me. They were hanging out in front of the corner liquor store, when they noticed me approaching. The store owners were from Yemen, and they displayed pictures of themselves holding AK-47 rifles in an attempt to scare us and keep us from stealing. As the boys walked towards me, I thought, "Wow, these guys are going to talk to me. Maybe they'll ask me to hang out with them."

When they encountered me, one of them asked, "Hey little vato, where you from?"

I told him, "Man! I ain't from nowhere. My mama said I can't be in the gang!"

He replied, "Oh yea? Well tell your mama this..." He punched me in the face. His friends ran up to me and begin to punch and kick me. I fell to the ground and curled up like a roly-poly bug. I was feared for my life. I thought that after kicking me in the stomach and head the guys would take a knife and finish me off. However, after a few kicks they decided to back off and return to their street corner.

The gang members walked a few yards to the liquor store and resumed talking to each other, like nothing had happened. I ran home and sat all day, in pain and crying, until my mother came home. "Mama, mama, the gangsters, los cholos, me brincaron, they jumped me!"

"Mi'jo, no seas menso, walk on the other side of the street!" she answered, frustrated. As much as I loved my mother, she sometimes did not have the right advice for me. She thought that the problems I encountered on the street were child's play, that I would be ok if I found ways to avoid these guys.

Maybe I couldn't avoid them, but it was more than that. What my mom did not realize was that the older gang members were a major influence in my life. I wanted to be like them because they had power, money, girls, and protection. I knew I shouldn't want this; I knew that it was irresponsible to join the gang. I confronted a paradox. On the one hand, I needed to avoid these gangsters in order to protect myself from failing in the future. On the other hand, these guys offered protection that no other group of people had ever offered me, not my teachers, not my mother, not the police.

My cousin, Pingo, had a connection to the gang. Pingo was my mother's brother's son. We were the same age, only a month apart. He was short, stubby, and, early on, by age 12, commanded respect with his thick voice and moustache, which he began growing when all of us, his cousins and friends, could only wish to have one. Pingo's uncle was one of the leaders of the gang, so Pingo had a connection, and could get us in with the older guys, the 17, 18, and

19-year-olds, the shot callers, if we were brave enough to pay them a visit. Here I was, age thirteen, and the gang life, "la vida loca," had come knocking at my door.

I'd already seen numerous shootings, people overdosing, and violent attacks, many of them gang-related. One day, when I was 11-years-old, I was standing in my front yard, having just finished a game of marbles with my neighbors, and a man in his 30's, whom I had never seen before, walked up to me. The man had a hard look; his eyes were slightly crossed and blood-shot. He was dirty, as if he had been on the streets for days without going home to sleep or shower. As he approached me, the man pulled out an enormous, shiny black gun. (Later on, as I experimented with different guns that I acquired from friends and gun dealers on the street, I estimated that the gun he pulled on me was a 9mm Glock pistol.) The stranger placed the gun on my forehead, the cold steel giving me an instant rush of goose bumps. Despite being scared, I felt a moment of letting go, of saying, "oh well, this is my moment." I relaxed my body, shrugged my shoulders and tilted my head up, as if inviting the guy to shoot.

He asked me "You a Northerner or a Southerner?" He wanted to know what affiliation I had to the two dominant Mexican prison gangs in California.

I told him, "I don't bang, man; I don't even know what you talking about." He looked at me cross-eyed and breathing heavily, and then he released the gun from my forehead and continued walking down the street.

I felt that what was left of my childhood was slowly being robbed from me. I knew that I did not want to live a life at-risk, full of trouble and violence. I decided to avoid these guys as much as I could. However, trouble continued to follow me. One day, as I followed my mother's suggestion and walked on the other side of the street, the same group of guys from before walked up to me and began to harass me. I thought to myself, "you got to be a man and handle your business."

The same guy who had punched me in the face a few weeks earlier came up to me and asked, "Where you from, ese?" I balled my fist up, lifted my arms, took a boxing stance, and started breathing heavily. The guys looked at me and laughed.

"What are you going to do?" one of them asked.

"Look at this little puto. He thinks he can hang with us!" another one exclaimed. I cocked my arm back, as if ready to throw a punch.

"Where you from, little vato?" one of them asked again.

I pointed at him, and replied, "I am from your 'hood.'"

"Oh, yeah?" he responded, and he began pounding on me like a boxer training on a punching bag.

With bruised ribs, bloody scrapes, and a throbbing headache, I limped to my cousin Pingo's house. I told him that I did not want to get beaten up and harassed any more, that I wanted some protection. Despite not wanting to join the gang, I felt that I had very little choice but to do so.

That night we took the bus to the liquor store parking lot, the "kick-it-spot," where the gang hung out. We walked up to Pingo's uncle, and told him we both wanted to get into the gang. He gathered a group of guys, and told us, "get ready."

Pingo's uncle, Maniac, began to talk.[1] My legs trembled under my extra baggy pants as he made the announcement, "You see these two lil' dudes? They are my nephews; they wanna' bang with us now. I want a couple of you fools to jump them in."

Before I knew it, there were five guys around me, and I knew I was going to get my ass kicked again, so I decided to take the first swing. Click! I hit the first guy in the jaw. I saw him look behind me, and, as I turned to see what he was looking at, I felt something hit me in the head. Hot flashes surrounded my cranium, and I fell to the ground. A skinny guy with fanged, canine-like teeth, nicknamed "Vampiro" [Vampire], mounted me. He smiled, showing me his fangs. He started punching me in the face. I blacked out. I later found out that one of the guys had kicked me in the head while I lay on ground.

Even though I was hurt, and had possibly suffered a concussion, I also felt tremendous joy. From now on, I would have power, money, girls, and protection. It was one of the most euphoric feelings I had ever felt. Moments after waking up, I was given a 40-ounce bottle of Old English Malt Liquor. I drank the pain

---

[1] In this book, I have changed some of the names of people, gangs, places, and neighborhoods for confidentiality purposes.

away by downing the entire "forty" in a matter of minutes. The homies welcomed me to the neighborhood, and quickly began to brainstorm a nickname for me.

"He looks sleepy, let's call him El Drowsy" one of them said.

"Chale homies, he hunches over like a puppet, let's call him El Puppet!" another one yelled.

Maniac responded, "Lil Puppet, that's your placaso [nickname]." I had arrived to the kick-it-spot empty handed, a no-name with nothing but a scrape on my forehead. I left that night with the power of the gang in my hands. I felt important.

A notorious gangster, an older homey who had been shot, stabbed, and imprisoned, once told me, during my first few months in the gang, as he took a puff of a giant marijuana blunt that looked like a fresh cut tree from a log forest, "We will always have new little homies because we make them feel important."

At that moment, I began to wonder, "Why is it that it takes a gang to make kids like me feel important? Why can't we feel important at school, or at a community center, or with the police?"

I never forgot this conversation. As a matter of fact, it was this question that would lead me to dedicate my life to finding an answer to it, "How can we help young people feel important, esteemed, and empowered, without having them participate in destructive behaviors?"

The night after I was jumped into the gang, I went over to the kick-it-spot, the dirt parking lot adjacent to the liquor store. Maniac and Conejo approached me. Maniac was a tall, dark guy with a big nose. He was a legend in Oakland; many knew him as a fierce fighter, beating the pulp out of his enemies. Conejo was a goofy-looking, pale, skinny man with big teeth, in his late 20's. They looked serious, ready to handle business. Conejo put his face half-an-inch from mine and said, "Look, puto, you need to prove yourself. I don't give a shit who you are, you better show me what you got."

Doing everything in my power not to show my fear, I replied, "What you want me to do?"

He said, "I want you to go down to 39th and cap one of those fucking fools."

I was afraid; I knew that if I got caught, I would face many years in prison. I also did not believe in killing people. I wanted to play the game, but I did not want the game to end with blood on my hands. I was torn, the little angel sitting on my left shoulder tried talking me into ignoring Conejo and disappearing, while the little devil sitting on my right shoulder whispered into my ear, telling me that if I backed

down now I would risk becoming the victim, and I would lose who, I thought, were the only friends I had. I thought to myself, "I got into this for a reason; I'm not goin' to back out now."
Conejo instructed me, "Let's go get a G-ride (stolen car), real quick."

We went to the hills of Oakland, where I'd gardened, and broke into a Chevrolet Iroc. I watched Conejo break the steering column with a screwdriver. He lifted up the ignition rod and the car purred. He drove off peeling rubber, swiftly getting us back to the kick-it-spot. As we arrived, one of the homies handed me a gun, a black .38 revolver with rust spots growing on it. I grabbed the gun, pretending to know how to use it. One of the guys handed me a forty. I drank half of it, and handed it over to another one of the guys. "Let's do this!" I told Conejo.

Conejo drove me to the rival territory. He spotted our enemies and told me, "There they go, let's get 'em." I grabbed the gun and pointed it towards the guys. Then, I raised the gun towards the air and shot into the night sky. The guys scattered like roaches and I fooled Conejo. I made him believe that I had shot at our rivals. However, I did not want to kill anyone so I decided to pretend to shoot at the guys. He thought I had shot to kill, when I had shot to intimidate. He was proud of me.

My reputation quickly grew. Even though I was one of the youngest guys in the gang, I got a lot of respect. While I knew that I might end up dead or locked up, the immediate gratification of feeling

47

empowered led me to continue putting in work on the streets. However, I did not realize how quickly the street life would catch up with me.

One day, about a year after having put in work stealing, fighting, building a reputation, and piling up a long list of rivals, my homies and I hung out at a Cinco de Mayo celebration at San Vicente Park in Oakland. I noticed that one of my enemies, a member of a rival gang whom I had fought with a few times, was hanging out with a group of his homeboys. I looked at him, and said to myself, "Here is my chance to get even with this puto for having jumped me the other day with his homeboys."

I quickly told all my homies, "I'm gonna' go fight this vato, back me up!" I walked towards him with a swarm of backup behind me; he had the same amount of backup. It seemed as if a giant mirror stood in front of me: my enemy's homeboys looked like a reflection of my homeboys; the same numbers, the same faces, the same skin color, even the same clothes, except different colors. I ran up on my rival and punched him, and fought him to the ground before the police came and broke us up.

Time slowed down. I felt a surge of power enter my body; my homies smiled at me, as if saying, "Good job, we're proud of you." I made a mortal enemy look like a chump in his own territory.

But, as I cleaned myself up, I noticed that my Oakland Raiders hat was missing, and I ran up the hill after our rivals. One of them had my hat on.

48

"Give me my hat!" I yelled out.

The guy looked back at me and said, "Chinga tu madre."

My homeboy, Rambo, walked up to the guy and demanded, "Give my homey his hat."
The guy responded by punching Rambo in the face. Rambo fell to the ground and started rolling downhill. When he picked himself up, he reached for a 12-inch knife that he had strapped to his waist. He ran up to the guy and stabbed him in the throat. The guy fell to the ground, holding his neck as the wound gushed uncontrollably. The more he opened his mouth, gasping for air, the more blood spurted. His tongue flip-flopped inside his mouth, as if it was a fish out of water. The guy died, and Rambo was arrested and sent to San Quentin State Penitentiary, where he is still serving a twenty-five-years to life sentence.

I felt badly for both guys. Our rival was dead for a trivial, petty, and worthless dispute, and Rambo had wasted his life for trying, too hard, to back up his homey. Every day for the past 18 years, I've thought about the lives of these two young men. I've thought about the long life of happiness they both could have had; I've thought about the kinds of careers they could have developed for themselves; I've thought about their families and how much they must miss them. I've also thought about my role in this tragedy. I've asked myself, many times, "If I would have done more to avoid the fight, would these two guys be alive and free today, enjoying the joys of life and the fresh air that freedom brings?"

At the time, having just turned 15, and already being deeply involved in the gang, I constantly shuffled between wanting to do good, to leave the gang, and to return to school, while, at the same time, I still continued to be involved in fights, stealing, and getting drunk and high on a routine basis. I believe that the reason I continued banging then was because I had yet to find an alternative to the lifestyle, one which could provide me with affirmation, security, and a healthy pastime.

Part of the gang life involved searching for my enemies and then challenging them to fights or jumping them. A few months after Rambo had been arrested for the murder, I was walking down the street in rival territory with three new recruits. I wanted to show them how to intimidate our enemies. I spotted one of our rival gang members inside a liquor store. I looked at my homeboys and said, "Look, homey, this is how you do it."

I grabbed a small, .25 caliber, semiautomatic gun from my pocket, clocked it, pointed it towards the back of the store where the liquor refrigerator stood, and unloaded it inside the store. My new recruits began to run; I yelled out at them to tell the to stop running. They stopped as I caught up to them. "There's no need to run," I explained, "the cops don't answer to gunshots for at least half an hour; we'll be at the homey's house by then."

I felt badly for terrifying the liquor store clerk and the innocent people who were in the store, but the thrill of proving my manhood and earning my stripes as a true, up-and-coming gangster covered up any feelings of empathy I had for others. I often reflect on this moment, and I believe that if there had been a healthy outlet for settling our disputes with other groups of boys.

Six years later, at the age of 20, after I had changed my life around, I returned to the store to apologize to the store owner and to ask how I could repay them back. The owner, an Asian man in his late 50's, recalled many incidents like this, committed by many people over the years. He told me that the best way to repay him was to find a way to stop the violence in the community. I promised him I would try. For weeks I hung out by the liquor store talking to the teenagers that lived in the area. I gained their respect and begin talking them into respecting the store. My reasoning was that the story was part of their neighborhood and that they needed to take care of what belonged to them. While I felt that I did not do much to repay the store owner for the madness I had imposed on him a few years earlier, at least I felt that I had influenced some of the young people in the neighborhood to respect the store.

We had walked about eight blocks, when, out of the blue, an old, white Toyota pulled up next to us. An older guy, around 20 years old, pulled out a shot-gun. He rested it on one arm, while he held the car's steering wheel with his other hand. The new recruits leaped over an old, wooden fence, like rabbits being chased by a fox. I knew that it was too late for me to hop the fence. There was only one thing I could do, drop to the ground as fast as I could. I heard the gunshot, less than 20 feet away; it was the loudest sound I had ever heard. The car drove off. As I got up, trying to make sense of what had just happened, I realized how close I had been to getting shot. I looked at the wooden staircase a few feet away from where I lay. Dozens of shotgun pellets had hit the steps. If my head had been 6 inches higher, I would have been hit.

The gang life had made me forget my morals, my obligations, and my sense of reality. I began to do the stupidest things to prove myself. At this moment, I was trying to figure out how to get revenge for my near death experience. I began to look for the guys who had called their older brother to come and shoot me.

Around then, my mother's boyfriend died. He was a bull rider at the local Mexican rodeos. Over time, he had fallen off enough vicious bulls to cause him fatal head trauma. I felt badly for my mother when her boyfriend died, but I was also happy. He had owned a 1982 Chevrolet Camaro, and had left my mother the keys, but she didn't drive. As my mother prepared for the funeral, I stole the keys to the car. I drove it to the kick-it-spot and began to brag.

My homies were excited. One of them, Grumpy, told me, "Let's go find the guys that tried to kill you!" A group of five of us each grabbed a "mini-bat" from my homeboy's house and went on a mission. As we strolled down Foothill Boulevard in Oakland, Grumpy, who was sitting in the passenger seat, spotted a guy and said, "That's him, that's one of the guys that tried to kill you, Puppet." I pulled the car over. Together, we all ran out of the car towards the guy. We did not even give him a chance to turn to look at us before we started hitting him with the mini-bats. He fell to the ground, screaming, and then Grumpy took a look at the guy's face. "Stop! Stop! Stop!" Grumpy yelled. "It's my primo! It's my cousin!"

With a puzzled look on my face, I turned to look at Grumpy, "What? What do you mean it's your cousin! You're the one that told us to kick his ass."

"Yeah, I couldn't tell, ay, it's my cousin."

We helped the boy stand up. "'Spensa [sorry], homey. We didn't know you were his cousin."

Looking back at these gangster days, I realize that in trying to flee from poverty and trauma, I had landed in a worse environment. I had put myself in a place where I had to pretend not to care for my life or the lives of other young people who looked and dressed just like me, my own people, separated by superficial colors and street names. Without the proper individuals to guide me, to make me feel empowered in healthy ways, I found a group of young people who had created a world where we could all feel powerful, even if it meant destroying our lives and the lives of others when we unleashed our power. I was traveling at the speed of light without any brakes. I felt that I was invincible and that if I did die or go to prison that was my destiny. Looking back at this mentality I recognize that my hopeless past of being a victim of poverty, neglect and violence had made me think this way. However, I did not realize at the time that I needed to find a way to turn these adversities into strengths, to make my life of struggle a reason for becoming successful. But all lies are eventually uncovered by the volcanic eruption of a truth. My crazy life was catching up to me and soon enough I would learn my lesson the hard way.

9

Juvenile Hall

You have the freedom to choose your actions;
you don't have the freedom to choose the
consequences of your actions.
-anonymous

One late night, at about 2 a.m. on a Saturday, my
cousin, Pingo, my homeboy, Pelon, and I were
driving to Oakland from San Francisco. We had paid
our homeboy, Mikey, a visit. Mikey was a crack
dealer in San Francisco. He had loads of money. My
16th birthday had passed a few days before, and I was
still celebrating. Mikey promised to take us all out to
eat some steak at a fancy, "white people's"
restaurant. We picked Mikey up in the Tenderloin
District, a neighborhood known for its homeless and
drug-addicted population. He was loitering in front
of a liquor store. As we pulled up, he threw up our
gang sign and jumped in the backseat through the
window. We drove to a steak restaurant on Pier 39.
I ordered the biggest steak in the house, a
porterhouse steak. The waiter asked me, "How
would you like it cooked?" I did not understand his
question, so I told him, "Just cook it man, cooked,
that's how I want it." He wanted to know if I wanted
the steak rare, medium-rare, medium, or well done.
I had been raised on Carne Asada, when we had

enough money to buy meat, and those cuts of steak are usually burnt to a crisp. The waiter assumed I would be happy with a medium-rare steak, what most steak connoisseurs believe to be the perfect temperature for the perfect steak. When I cut into the steak, I saw blood dripping onto my plate and oozing into my mashed potatoes. I dropped my knife, and almost threw up. I called the waiter and reminded him that I wanted my steak cooked, not raw.

Years later, when I worked as a waiter at a steakhouse to pay my way through college, I learned about the different cuts of meats and their optimal temperatures. Looking back, I realize how limited my understanding of mainstream culture was, and how my friends and I had never had a chance to learn about the larger society around us. Today, every time I order a steak, usually medium-rare, I laugh at the time when I was repulsed by a perfectly cooked steak. However, I would never give up my taste for the crispy Carne Asada that I grew up eating.

After gorging on pounds of extra well-done steaks, paid for by Mikey's crack money, we dropped him off at the liquor store. As we crossed the San Francisco Bay Bridge into Oakland, I noticed a weird, burning smell. I told the guys, "Hey man, do you smell that? Maybe the car is burning."

Half asleep with his eyes closed, Pelon turned my way and told me, "Don't worry about it, man, we'll check it when we get to my house."

We drove for a few more miles. The car started spewing smoke from under the hood. Only a few blocks away from Pelon's house, I decided to keep driving. As we pulled up into Pelon's driveway, a huge cloud of black smoke spewed from under the hood. I got out of the car and noticed that flames were lapping out. "Get some water!" I yelled at the guys. Pelon returned with a bucket; Pingo with a hose. I opened the hood, and a fireball rolled out of the car. The guys attacked the flames with water.

Overwhelmed by the smoke fumes and the fact that I would no longer have a car to drive, I ground my teeth. Suddenly, I heard gunshots. Turning towards Pingo, I wondered if he started to shoot his gun off into the air, out of frustration. As I turned in his direction, Pingo leapt into the air, and the water hose flew in the opposite direction. At this point, I realized that we were under attack. I lunged towards the front of my burning car. Pingo and Pelon emerged from the smoke. None of us had been shot, but my car was out of commission.

The Camaro was a wreck. I needed a new ride. A few days after my car burned, my homeboy, Psycho, asked me if I wanted to drive a car he had stolen. I told him I wanted the car, but that I also wanted him to teach me how to steal cars. A few days after rolling around in the stolen car, I was pulled over and arrested by the police. One officer took me into a small interrogation room. He told me, "Listen, if you want the judge to take it easy on you, you have to write a letter of apology for stealing the car."

"O.k." I replied. I wrote a letter: "I am sorry to the owner of the car. I needed a car because mines burnt down." What I did not realize was that by forcing me to write a letter of apology, the officer was essentially guaranteeing my admission to having committed the crime. Later, my lawyer told me that there was nothing she could do to help me, since I had admitted guilt.

The officer left me in the interrogation room for hours. I noticed the name of a rival gang written on the wall. I grabbed the pen that I had used to write my letter, and scratched the name out. Then I wrote, "El Puppet," and the name of my gang. The officer walked in the room and told me, "That's what I wanted. Now you just gave me your gang and your nickname." He took pictures of me and of the three-dot tattoo on my left hand. He then filled in a "gang card" that contained all of my information as a gang member. These kinds of corrupt police tactics were common experiences for my homies and me. While many of us had committed crimes that deserved punishment, we were often entrapped by police, sometimes for transgressions we did not commit.

Classified as a gang member and found guilty before having the option to plead innocent, I was headed to a jail cell. The officer dropped me off with the juvenile hall guards. One of them searched me, gave me a change of clothes, and told me to go take a shower. Afterwards, he made me rub a bunch of grease into my hair. "That's for in case you got lice or some other nasty shit on you," he said. The guard walked me to a tiny cell. I walked in. A cold cement bed awaited me. Next to it was a stainless steel toilet and a small sink. He handed me a thin cushion and a slim blanket. Slam! The door shut behind me. I was alone. No homies, no family, no warmth.

The next day, after a rough night's sleep, I woke up to the guard's shouting, "Rios! Wake up." I walked to the door, thinking that I would be released to go to the yard. "Na, na, na, stay in there. Here's your breakfast." Slam! The door shut again. I looked at my breakfast. Two small pieces of egg, the size of poker chips, lay on the plate. A piece of brown toast, stale and stiff, accompanied the eggs. "Juice! Juice!" I thought, and then noticed a small container, the kind that restaurants use to put salad dressing in, with a cap on it. I uncovered the container, savoring the small gulp of juice I was about to have. As I pulled off the lid, I noticed a big green loogie, a large slimy glob of spit, mixed with nose snot, floating in my apple juice.

While the juvenile facility was attempting to scare me into leaving the street life behind by making my life miserable while doing time, it only created more hate in my heart. Juvi had set up a game for me to play, I would try to outsmart them and not get caught and they would try to lock me up again and make sure they made my life miserable. This viscous cycle only made the streets more crime ridden and violent because the boys who went to juvi learned to become bigger and harder criminals while they were locked away. As I played the game I ran the risk of being tagged and eventually charged for gang conspiracy or a crime to benefit the gang. These charges carried long sentences like 5, 10, 15 or 25 years in prison. The crazy thing was that may of my homies who were locked away for all those years had not committed those crime or had not even been present but the fact that they had been tagged as gang members by police had led them to prison. I was quickly setting my self up to be locked away for an eternity; I was preparing for prison.

10

A Home For My Homey

> If there is no struggle, there
> is no progress.
> -Fredrick Douglas

After being released from "juvi," having spent a few days incarcerated, I began to hang out with a childhood friend, Smiley, whom I had convinced to join the gang. I felt big and bad, knowing that I had done some "time." I felt that my friends respected me more for spending time locked away. When I got released, Smiley went to look for me at my house. He wanted to know everything there was to know about juvi. He wanted to know who was there, if I had gotten into a fight, and what I had learned.

Smiley was a naïve kid, beaten by his parents. But no matter how bad his circumstances were—homeless, victimized, or hungry—he always kept a radiant grin on his face. His smile got him into trouble. When he smiled in class, the teacher thought he was laughing at her. He smiled when he didn't understand what was going on in class, and when the teacher yelled at him. I remember one time, when we were hanging out on one of our gang's street corners on International Boulevard, rival gang members drove by, shooting at us, and, as I turned to

63

tell Smiley to run, I could see he was looking at them with a big smile.

Smiley was an innocent kid, but he lived in the wrong place to be that way. He was seen as a problem kid in school, and spent many of his school days in the detention room. On the street, police often stopped him as he walked home from school, even before he joined the gang, because, from their perspective, the baggy clothes he wore marked him as a gang member. I was present many times when this happened. I'd already joined the gang, but not Smiley. The police still treated him like the rest of us. He was followed around, searched, handcuffed, and harassed. Over time, Smiley came to think of the gang as his only source of support.

I joined the gang seeking the protection that I thought police and other authority figures in my community had failed to provide. Smiley wanted to join for similar reasons. When he was fourteen, we offered to jump him into the gang. He agreed, and that same night we took him to the side of Pelon's garage, where, next to an abandoned white refrigerator, a group of about eight of us punched him in the face, slammed him to the ground, and kicked him in the stomach. One of the homies grabbed a tall umbrella and hit him with it until the umbrella's aluminum structure collapsed and the fabric ripped off. After a few minutes, we picked him up, gave him hugs, and handed him an "8 ball," a forty ounce bottle of Old English Malt Liquor. He was officially one of us, part of our "familia," our "street family."

Smiley became my best friend. When his parents permanently kicked him out of the house, I told him not to worry. "I'm going to find you a home," I said. That night, I stole a 1980's Oldsmobile Cutlass Supreme, breaking the steering column with a large, heavy-duty, flat head screwdriver to gain access to the ignition rod. I drove it to our neighborhood, walked up to Smiley, handed him the screwdriver, and told him, "Here's your new two bedroom apartment." Referring to the front and rear seats, I joked, "I'll sleep in the front room and you sleep in the back room."

A few days later, I was pulled over by the police again for driving this stolen car. When I stopped in the parking lot of a large drug store on the intersection of Fruitvale Avenue and Foothill Boulevard in East Oakland, the cops dragged me out of the car, knocked me on my back, and repeatedly kicked me in the stomach and legs. I remember yelling like a little boy: "Awww! Help! Awww! Help!"

The officer kicking me shouted back, "Shut the fuck up! You want to be a criminal, then you're going to get treated like one!" He stomped my face against the ground with his thick, black, military-grade, rubber boots, his shoes' soles leaving scrapes and gashes on my upper lip and cheek bone. I was fourteen-years-old.

After the beating, I was taken to "One-fitty," the name we had given the juvenile justice facility in our county because it was located on 150th Avenue. This time, while doing time, a boy I met by the name of Tony taught me how to sand down a 1980s Honda car key to convert it into a master key for all early 1980s Hondas. The day after my release, I got hold of a 1980s Honda key, scraped it on the cement over the course of a few hours, went to a BART station parking lot, and stole another car to pick up Smiley and "go cruising." No matter how many times I got arrested, or how much time they had me spend in juvenile hall, I kept stealing cars.

Looking back, I realize that I had a one-track mentality. I believed that I was destined to go to prison, that I was not going to survive to the age of 18, that I was a good- for-nothing criminal. This attitude led me to commit acts that put me at risk. If I had known a better world was possible, that one day I could lift my family out of poverty, that my attitude was not the only way I could solve my problems, I would have stopped committing crimes. However, no one had taught me an alternative way to deal with my obstacles. I would have to learn through one of the most brutal lessons a human being could experience.

11

Smiley's Death

The Best Revenge is Massive Success.
                    -Frank Sinatra

One day, Smiley, Big Joe and I visited some girls we
had met. They lived in a neighborhood where many
of our rival gang members lived. When we arrived,
we spotted the girls sitting on their front porch. As
we began talking with them, we noticed that a group
of about eight rival gang members were walking
down the street towards us. We were all about the
same age, fourteen to seventeen years old, and all
dressed the same: baggy, creased up, Ben Davis or
Dickies brand work pants, with tucked-in, white t-
shirts or baggy sports jerseys. The only difference
was that we wore different colors to represent our
gang affiliations.

Apparently, word had gotten out that we were
intruding into their neighborhood. They recognized
us from previous fights we had had with them over
the past few months. Trying to prove our toughness,
we threw up our gang signs and called them out for a
one-on-one fight. Their plan was different. They
wanted to gang up on us and beat us down. Once
they reached us, they surrounded us, and we began
to fight. I fell down a few times, and the last time I

got up, one of them pulled out a gun. I ran. Hearing gunshots, I leaped between two cars for protection. I turned back, our enemies faded away as they scattered behind apartment buildings. I checked my body for blood to see if I had been shot. I was fine. I found Big Joe lying on the ground. He stood up and told me he was fine. We looked for Smiley. He was nowhere in sight. I turned the corner on the car I had hidden behind. There was Smiley, face flat on the ground. I ran over to him, kneeling over his body and grabbing him, trying to get him to stand up. Smiley had been shot. The bullet had hit him in the head.

Fresh, human blood painted a picture of death on my white Nike Cortez shoes. I stood on that dark street knowing that Smiley was dying. I thought, as the movies had taught me, that he should have been dead the instant the bullet hit his skull, but he continued to twitch and shake as we drove him to the hospital. We'd decided not to call an ambulance; we knew from previous experience that it wouldn't arrive in time. In the past, we had been told by law enforcement that standard procedure dictated that the police had to clear a crime scene before an ambulance could move in, and we had lost many friends and relatives to this policy. The ambulance often took over 45 minutes to arrive when someone was shot in my neighborhood. A few hours later at the hospital, Smiley was declared dead.

The police told me that it was my fault that my homeboy had died, and threatened to arrest me for being present at the shooting, with a charge of accessory to murder. I asked them if they were "going to catch the murderer."

"What for?" one of the officers replied, "We want you to kill each other off."

I didn't want to let Smiley's death pass without revenge. The laws of the street stated that I had to retaliate for what had happened to my homey. A few days after Smiley's death, a few of my homies and I drove up to our hang-out spot and opened the hood to the car. Three guns were stashed away in various corners between the fender and the engine. I got excited. This was my chance to hurt those who had killed my best friend.

As I got ready to jump into the car, I remembered what the cop had told me. He wanted us to kill each other off. He thought, as many other police officers did, that we were trash, and that it would be best if we served as our own garbage disposal service, and, that way, he would not have to deal with us anymore. I began to think about my dead homey, and I asked myself, "What would Smiley want me to do?" I knew that Smiley would not want me to end up in prison, nor would he want me to kill another young man who looked like us, talked like us, and dressed like us, with only colors and neighborhood names differentiating us. I told the guys that I could not go with them, that I needed time. They called me a coward, and told me that I wasn't down for the neighborhood. Despite their pressure, I resisted joining them in their cruise of death. So, my homies decided to go without me. They shot up our rivals' neighborhood. Later on the police found them and arrested them. They are still doing time in prison today.

Smiley's death forced me to reflect on my life. I was torn; I did not want to end up dead or incarcerated. Even though I had lost most of my faith, I had a small crumb of hope that I could still do something positive with my life. At the same time, I was ready to go and get revenge; I wanted to shoot up the guys who had killed my homey.

Where would I turn for guidance? Who would help me with this life-altering decision? I decided to go to the one person who had told me that she would be there for me when I wanted to turn my life around. I went to my teacher.

12

Ms. Russ

The mediocre teacher tells. The good
teacher explains. The superior teacher
demonstrates. The great teacher inspires.
-William Arthur Ward

One day, I returned to school after a long hiatus, and
I looked for Ms. Russ. By this time, I had dropped at
least one semester in the eighth grade, one in the
ninth grade, and now, one in the tenth grade. In the
eighth grade, I had gone to work, but in the ninth
and tenth grades, I was on the streets of Oakland
hanging out, selling drugs, and stealing and robbing.
I thought that I could never make it through school,
that I was too stupid, and that the streets were a
place where I did know how to survive and make
money. I felt that even though I risked being
murdered, going to jail, or ending up a drug-addict,
like many of the people I knew, the streets had more
to offer me than school did.

My mother knew that I was getting into trouble. She
knew that I was not doing well in school, and that I
was hanging out with trouble-makers. However, she
never found out that I was in the gang, or how deeply
I was involved in violence, crime, and drug abuse. I
did everything that I could to hide my bad ways from
my mother and my siblings. I did not want them to
know that I was a thug who was giving a bad name

73

to our family. In addition, my mother had too much going on to be in touch with what I was going through. She worked full-time, cleaning up the salad bar at Sizzlers Restaurant, and, by this time, she was single again, and had just lost custody of my little brother, Mike, and my little sister, Rosa, for neglecting them. My older brother, J.T., had gotten fed up with our mother's alcoholism and had moved out of the house. J.T. had confronted her for her irresponsibility and my mother had told him off, ordering him to leave the house and never come back.

My mother went out to bars almost every night to drink her pain away. Alone, and not having anyone to turn to at home, I felt as if I was also killing myself. "I'd rather be dead," I thought. During this rock bottom time in my life, as I continued my destructive path with even more intensity and hate, I remembered the one person who had told me that she would be there for me if I needed someone to talk to. I went back to school to look for Ms. Russ.

As I was walking down the hallway, Ms. Russ opened her classroom door and noticed me. Her eyes lit up with joy. "Why is this crazy lady so happy?" I asked myself, "Every time I see her she has a big smile on her face! I want to be on whatever she's been smoking!"

Ms. Russ walked up to me and said, "Victor, are you O.K.? I heard what happened."

Trying to be a tough guy, I responded, "Yeah, I'm O.K." as I bowed my head and balled my fists up.

She reached over, tapped me on the shoulder, and said, "Victor, I know you are not O.K. Listen to me, I am here for you."

At this moment, I felt all the pain, all the anger, all the fear that had been building up in me move from my stomach to my chest, and, finally, through my eyes. I began to cry like a little kid, in front of the entire school during passing time. A group of students gathered around me. I was embarrassed. Ms. Russ opened her arms, gave me a hug, and told me that if I was ready to turn my life around, she would be there to support me, but that I had to do the work. She told me that she would guide me and advocate for me, but, again, that I would have to be ready to put in the time and the work.

While I was still tempted to go back to the streets, to hide out with my homies, to avoid the stress of going back to the classroom and feeling stupid and bored there, I also knew that it was time to change. I got this feeling in my heart, this tingling, that told me that I should improve my life, that if I did not do it for myself, I should at least do it for Smiley who was dead, for my little brother and sister who were with their father and needed a good role model, for my mother, who even though she had neglected me, had risked her life and broken her back to feed and clothe me. I knew that this was the moment to change, because I had finally found the right person to help me. If a teacher told me that she would be there for me, that she would support me, then I no longer had the excuse that I had no one to guide and help me. I don't think Ms. Russ will ever know the profound impact that her words and brief hug had in my life. I was seeking someone to provide a small flame so that I could begin to light the fire of transformation, and Ms. Russ approached me at the right moment to fire me up.

I believe that young people who are placed at risk are like oysters--they rarely open up. We never know when a young person will be ready to change, when he or she will open up. Therefore, it is important to provide a steady and constant stream of guidance, opportunity, and unconditional nurturing, so that when that young person is ready to change, when he or she finally opens up, he or she can find the resources to do so. I also had to learn to receive help from others. I realized that opportunity is hard to come by so when a person lends a helping hand one needs to open his arms up and embrace that support. It takes two to tango and a young person who struggles needs the support to make it to the next level, however, this same young person needs to hold himself accountable for his actions and correct his own mistakes, ask for forgiveness, and learn to make things better in his life.

I took on Ms. Russ's challenge. She began to guide me; I accepted responsibility for my actions, stayed in class during lunch and after school to make up my credits, and enrolled in night school. This is the deal we made: I would keep trying, and her belief in me would not waiver. Ms. Russ also advocated for me with administrators, teachers, and probation officers, making sure that they gave me a second chance as well.

Ms. Russ believed in me so much that she tricked me into believing in myself. She knew that I was behind in reading. She knew I could barely read at a sixth-grade level. One day, during her class, she handed me a copy of Shakespeare's Othello, an impossible book for me to read. With a serious look in her eyes, she told me, "Take this book home and try it out." I did, but after browsing through a few complex passages, feeling confused, and getting a big headache, I decided Ms. Russ was wrong to give me this assignment. I had no idea what Shakespeare was talking about. However, in a way, Ms. Russ was right. While I was not able to understand many of the things I read, she helped me to gain confidence in myself. She helped me understand that with patience and time, I could read even the most difficult books one day. I must admit, though, that even today, with a Ph.D. and all of my education, I still get a headache trying to read Shakespeare. But now, if I want to, I can read any of his books and be able to decipher his language.

It took me awhile to change. Upon returning to

school at the end of my sophomore year, I got into a few fights and cussed out a few teachers. But, by the beginning of my junior year, I was much more mature and fully ready to change. I had to make many sacrifices to do so. The first week of junior year, one of my enemies at school came up to me and called me a "pendejo" [idiot]. He pushed his shoulder into me as he walked past me. A group of students witnessed the event. Instead of following my instinct to punch him in the face, I gave him a dirty look and walked away. I felt that I needed to challenge myself and be willing to let go of some of my pride if I was going to successfully catch up on my credits and earn my high school diploma. From this day onward, the guys who did not like me at school called me "coward," "punk," "pussy," and "sissy." These names hurt. I felt as if I had lost control of my life. Thinking back, if I would have reacted to these negative remarks, I would have gotten myself into more trouble, and would probably have been kicked out of school or arrested. I wouldn't have made it to where I am today. Despite wanting to smash their faces in, I ignored their remarks and told myself that I would not get into a fight unless I was being physically attacked.

Ms. Russ was patient with me. She knew that it would take awhile for me to turn my life around. No matter how bad I was, or how many times I got kicked out of school, she always welcomed me back to her classroom after I had paid my dues. She did not show rancor or fear. She knew that if she was going to help make a change in my life, she had to have faith that I could redeem myself and learn to interact with a teacher. She treated all of the students with the same respect. Some teachers at my school gave special treatment to students who received good grades, not Ms. Russ. Whenever anyone of us got out of line, she disciplined us equally. Whenever anyone of us accomplished a task, she rewarded us, even if that task was somewhere below our grade level.

One other crucial practice was that Ms. Russ understood her students' social situations. She took the time to understand each of our individual worlds by meeting our families, getting to know them, and seeing where we were from. She understood our struggles. For example, one day while we hung out in front of our apartment complex on a Sunday afternoon, Ms. Russ drove up. We lived in what we called "the ghetto apartments." This was where most of the "bad" kids at the school lived, and it was bad. The place was notorious for violence and drug abuse, and it was far from Ms. Russ's "nice," middle-class neighborhood. But, despite the fear that people had created about our complex, Ms. Russ took the time and the care to pay us a visit.

As she drove up in an white, late model Honda Civic, I looked at my two homeboys who sat on the curb with me, and said, "Get up, get up, Ms. Russ is here. Give her some respect!" We all stood up, dusted our pants, and gave Ms. Russ big smiles of greeting. She walked up to us and said hello.

"Are your parents home?" she asked.

"Are we in trouble?" I said.

"Not at all. I just came by to say hello to your parents. Is that o.k.?"

Ms. Russ walked up to my apartment door and knocked, and when my mother opened the door she said, "Hola." That was the only word in Spanish my teacher knew. "Hello," my mom responded. That was one of the few words in English my mother knew. Despite the language barrier, Ms. Russ made an effort to talk to my mother with my little sister Rosa, who was visiting for the weekend, to translate for her. "Tell your mom your brother is not in trouble," she told my sister, "I am just here to say hello and see how everyone is doing." This short, twenty-minute visit to see our families once a semester went a long way.

Ms. Russ understood that in order to teach young people who had given up on school, she had to gain their trust and respect. She knew she had to ask our permission to teach us. Other teachers had the opposite expectation; they wanted us to ask their permission to learn from them. We resisted, and in doing so, a lose-lose educational environment was created. The key to success for Ms. Russ was showing us respect and expecting respect from us in return. She believed in us, and she knew that we had to give our consent before she would be able to teach and support us.

My teacher, Ms. Russ, saved my life. She taught me how to take my struggles and turn them into my strengths. She inspired me to believe in myself so that I could imagine myself accomplishing the unbelievable. With the help of my teacher I stopped making excuses for my failures and began to set myself up for success. During this time Ms. Russ reminded me of a saying, "when you fail to plan, you plan to fail." It was at this moment that I realized that for the first 16 years of my life I did not know what it meant to plan and this had led me to failure. I was living life hoping to live just another day, or until the age of 18, but now I had to think 5 and 10 years ahead. I drew out a plan for myself, a vision chart, showing where I would be 5 years from now, 10 years from now, and I did not allow myself to put any negative things on it. I wrote on this board that in 10 years I would own my own house, I would have a college degree, I would have a good paying job, and that I would have children and be a good father to them. Ten years later, at the age of 26, I had accomplished all of this and much more. Planning for a 5 to 10 year future can be a powerful tool. Picking up a pen and a piece of paper at the age of 16 became a huge payoff for me. Every word I wrote mapping out my future became a prophecy, an accurate prediction for the bright successful life I would began to live after leaving my fatalistic mentality behind.

13

College

Some of us are late bloomers,
but spectacular when we flourish.
- Dr. Victor Rios

By the time I was ready to graduate, I had brought
up my grade point average from 0.9 to 1.9. I was
encouraged by college student mentors and by Ms.
Russ to apply to college. I thought they were crazy.
But Ms. Russ insisted, and asked some college
students to give me a tour of UC Berkeley. They
convinced me to apply to a state school where I
would have a chance of being accepted, despite my
low grade point average.

Even though I had a 1.9 G.P.A., I had raised my
grades from F's and D's to B's and A's. Ms. Russ
told me that the university would take this into
account and would consider me a "late bloomer,"
someone who had started slower than others but who
would eventually catch up. I applied to one school,
California State University, Hayward. A few months
later, when I received a letter of acceptance, I
thought I was dreaming.

The letter informed me that I would be admitted on
probation. I was ready for that. I pictured some
police officer following me around to my classes at
the university. I already had a probation officer from
being locked up in Juvi so I told myself, "Probation?

I am already on probation, so that won't matter."
Luckily, I was mistaken. I did not know that, in
college, probation meant I would be expelled if I
received below a C average.

University life was one of the most exciting times of
my life. During the summer, before starting classes,
I lived on campus in university dorms, where I
attended a program known as Upward Bound. This
program was created to help young people who had
not received the proper academic training to improve
their writing and mathematics skills prior to their
first year of college. In the dorms, I had to share a
tiny room with another male student. His name was
Duc; he was a Vietnamese American student who
was also from Oakland. Duc's parents had come to
the United States after the Vietnam War. Duc told
me that U.S. soldiers had gone into his parents
village and killed many of his male relatives. His
village was then burned down. His parents managed
to escape and eventually were able to come to the
United States as refugees.

Duc also struggled while growing up in Oakland. He
was constantly punked and challenged by Latino and
African American boys. He became fed up with the
bullying and created a gang with other Asian
American youth. Duc eventually went to juvi,
witnessed crazy violence, changed his life, and ended
up in college, too. Duc and I talked about our
common struggles and wondered why our people,
despite being from such different parts of the world,
had to suffer so much.

Our room was so tiny, it barely held our two beds and two desks. Neither of us could stand being in our room at the same time. We took turns being there during the day, and would only go into the room at night to sleep. The dorms had a cafeteria that served food buffet style, all you can eat. The first week I was really excited, knowing that I could eat all the food I wanted. I had spent my childhood wondering if there would be enough food to eat when I got home from school and now my quandary was figuring out which of the many foods to choose from.

However, within four weeks, I got fed up with eating the same mundane dorm food: hard tator tots, soggy eggs, and dry toast for breakfast; cold pasta, sour spaghetti sauce, and stale garlic bread for lunch; and wet chicken breast, frozen peas and carrots, and tasteless mashed potatoes for dinner. But I was there to study and get my college degree, not to eat gourmet food.

I could not believe that, in college, I only had to go to classes two or three days a week. And, on the days I attended classes, I only had to be there for less than 2 hours per class. However, the classes were extremely difficult. I could barely understand what the professor talked about, and his big words, like "epistemology" and "Postmodernism," made me feel self-conscious and stupid. I felt like I would never be able to understand all the big college talk. But, I did all that I could to hang on. Every time I did not understand a big word, I would write it down, and, at night, I would grab the dictionary and look the word up. Little by little, with patience and dedication, I began to understand some of the vocabulary that my professors and classmates were using. I started to feel less stupid, and I began to believe that I actually belonged in college.

I failed a few classes during my first two quarters in college, and almost got kicked out of school. However, I convinced administrators that I would catch up, that I would go to all the tutoring programs on campus, and that I would bring up my grades. I studied until 3 a.m. every night, staying awake by drinking 4-5 cups of coffee. Over time, my grades begin to pick up, and, by my second year, my transition into college was in full motion.

College was such a different world from where I came from. People were focused; no one fought; I did not have to watch my back wherever I walked; and everyone there had one common goal: to work hard, get through college, and acquire a 4-year Bachelor's Degree. If, in high school, I had felt trapped having to stay in school for seven hours a day, five days a week, in college, I felt all the freedom in the world.

After getting the hang of college, I decided that it was time for me to move back home to my old neighborhood, to help my mother with the bills, and to help her raise my brother Mike and sister Rosa; she had just regained custody of them and they needed a lot of help. 14-year-old Mike was involved in the street life, going to juvi, and even becoming addicted to crack cocaine. 12-year-old Rosa was starting to get into boys, and was defiant to my mother. I started to take them both to community meetings where people talked about community service and political organizing. I also introduced them to Aztec Dancing, an ancient tradition that our ancestors in Mexico practiced for thousands of years. Eventually, we all learned to connect to our past, in order to improve our futures. Over time, Mike left his addiction behind, and Rosa finished high school, despite deciding to get married and have a baby at 17. Today, Mike is a mechanic and the father of two kids. He is an excellent father, very connected to both of his kids. Rosa is the mother of three kids, is married to a successful roofing contractor, and works as an administrative assistant at a successful business. My older brother J.T. eventually earned his Engineering degree from San Jose State University. He is a father of two, a good family man, and he works as an Engineer for the City of Livermore, California.

14

Ancient Tradition

To forget one's ancestors is to be a brook
without a source, a tree without root.
-Chinese proverb

During college, I began to tutor and mentor high school students. I wanted to help other young people who lived in poverty and needed guidance and support to make it to college. I believed that if people like my teacher and mentors were there to help me out, I needed to do my part and help other young people as well. I started the Carnalitas Carnalitos [Little Sisters Little Brothers] mentoring program at local schools in Hayward, Oakland, and Berkeley. Beyond wanting high school students to do well in school, I also wanted to help them learn about their cultures, their ancestors, their traditions. We began to have discussions about what it meant to be a Latino in the United States, what it meant to be Indigenous people from the Americas who had lost their powerful traditions, and in what ways we could learn from our ancestors.

No matter our heritages, people are like trees, without roots, they fall over. I believe that everyone should have a clear understanding of history. In this manner, we don't repeat the mistakes of others, and we recover positive traditions that have been lost.

For example, in many Indigenous traditions from the Americas, women took a central role in leadership. They were respected. Women were not called "bitches" and "hos" and seen as objects for men to take advantage of. Some of these societies were matriarchal; women called the shots; they were the leaders, and they told the men how to run government and organize their lives. According to some historians, matriarchal societies had less war, better living conditions, and more prosperity because of the balanced way in which women were treated. Unfortunately, European invaders, starting 500 years ago and continuing to the present day, attempted to erase Indigenous peoples' knowledge, ways of governing, and spirituality. They chose to believe that our ancestors were inferior heathens and devil worshipers, and they began to violently teach the Indigenous people how to be more like Europeans, forcing them to take on European names—like "Rios," a name from Spain—and to follow European religion and tradition, including the idea that women were inferior, that men were superior, and that women were to be treated as objects. Learning this history made me want to recover the past so that I could help to create a better future for my children and their children. I learned that in many Indigenous cultures individuals were taught to live their lives planning for seven generations in the future.

I also became part of a group of Aztec Dancers, "Danzantes." I learned that Danza Azteca is not a dance. It is a form of prayer; it is a form of learning about the universe. The dancers, in all their beautiful feathers and amazing sounding chachayotes that they place on their ankles, dance around the drum. The drum represents the sun and the dancers represent the planets making gravitational orbits around the center that holds them together. I learned that the Danza was used as a form of building community, teaching young people about the cosmos and society, and as a form of medicine.

When I came to Danza, I was in pain. When I was a freshman, I had watched the murder of my uncle Dario. At my goddaughter's first birthday party, in the driveway of my home, some guys from next door had called out my mom's brother for a fight. My mother and I walked with my 22-year-old uncle, to try to stop him from fighting. As my uncle walked up to the guy who had called him out to fight, the guy pulled out a gun. My mother stood on one side of my uncle, while I stood on another. The guy walked up to my uncle, raised the gun to his head, and shot him, point blank in the head. My uncle died instantly.

After my uncle's death, my whole family needed healing and a place to vent their pain. A few days later, we went to the Aztec Dancers for support. They took us in, and taught my siblings and eight of my younger cousins the ancient traditions from thousands of years ago. They taught us that the smoke that burns in the center of the circle was there for us to put our prayers into; that smoke would carry to the heavens and help us alleviate the pain. They taught us different dances, like the Deer Dance,

the Warrior Dance, and the Eagle Dance. Each of
these dances represented a certain aspect of life, of
struggle, what we sought answers for.

Motivated by the beauty of my ancestors and the
healing powers that they left behind, I became an
active Danzante in the circle, and brought many
young people whom I worked with to benefit from
learning about our traditions. The group we danced
for was named Cuahtonal, meaning "Fire Eagle" in
Nahuatl, one of the main languages of the
Indigenous peoples of Mexico. By 1998, I was
honored by three Danza groups in the San Francisco
Bay Area, Cuahtonal, Xipetotec, and Xitlalli, for my
service to the community. They gave me the
Cuahtemoc Award, an award given to someone who
personifies the spirit of the last Aztec emperor.
Cauhtemoc helped his people, and protected his
culture and history, during violent attacks by the
Spanish. The Spanish soldiers captured him and
began to burn him alive; they tried to force him to
tell them where the people's treasures and gold were
hidden. Cauhtemoc refused to talk, and instead sent
a message to all of his people to remind them to
shelter and save the traditions, the real treasure,
until the violent attacks went away:

> ...Our Sun has gone down. Our Sun has been
> lost from view and has left us in complete
> darkness. But we know it will return again ...
> let's embrace each other and in the very center
> of our being hide all that our hearts love and
> we know is the Great Treasure. Let us hide our
> Temples, our schools, our sacred soccer game,

our youth centers, our houses of flowery song, so that only our streets remain. Our homes will enclose us until our New Sun rises.

Cuahtemoc's message inspires me everyday. It reminds me that the real treasure is that of keeping our families together, of helping our communities heal, and of making this world a better place by leading by example. It is our responsibility to teach others, those who solve their problems through violence and war, to manage our world in healthier and more sustainable ways. Ancient traditions hold part of the answer to make this world a better place. It is our mandate to recover these traditions, no matter what part of the world we are from, and learn from them. Aztec Dance helped me heal. It helped me ground myself, and it served as a place for me to strengthen my spirit so that I could continue on my journey to help other young people like me. I was so compelled by Danza Azteca that I danced for 10 years. Eventually, I injured my knee and had to take a break. But the drum beats in my heart everyday.

15

Dream Job

Ain't no power like the power
of the youth 'cause the
power of the youth don't stop!
-Youth Activists' Chant

After four tough but fun years in college, I graduated
with a Bachelor of Arts Degree in Human
Development with an Emphasis in Adolescent
Development. Graduating from college was the most
amazing experience of my life so far. I felt that now I
could officially consider myself an adult, a man. I
could use this degree to get a good paying job, and
then I could take care of my family and myself. If,
as I teenager, I had felt trapped, with no purpose in
life, now, as a college graduate, I felt free and
successful. The graduation ceremony was
exhilarating. My mother, siblings, and girlfriend
attended. I sat in the middle of the school's football
stadium, where the graduation was held. A keynote
speaker talked about her experiences growing up
poor in the American South, and how she had now
become vice-president of A.T. & T. She said that she
was happy to live in a house with three toilets now,
because as a kid she was so poor that she lived in a
shack with no toilet. I told myself that one day, with
the college degree I was handed, I wanted to buy

myself a house that had hot water, because as a kid there were times when our water heater was broken and we did not have warm water to take showers.

My family could not believe that I was finally done with school. They were so proud of me. It was at this moment that I proved to them I could go from being on the streets and in juvi, to becoming a successful adult, a responsible man who could eventually support himself and his family.

A few months before graduating, I applied for a job as a Gang Prevention Counselor at a middle school in Berkeley, California. I was called in for an interview. Two teachers asked me questions for over an hour. "What makes you qualified for this job?" they asked. I was nervous and had to take deep breathes and do lots of thinking to answer their questions. Fortunately, college was preparing me well. I used some of the big vocabulary I had learned in my college classes to answer their questions. I also told them my personal story of being involved in gangs. They admired the fact that I had come from two worlds; I had survived the streets, and I was on the verge of successfully completing my college education. I have found that in the educational field, and in mainstream society, people respect and admire my story. Many people tell me that I have an American Dream story, a Horatio Alger story, of coming from poverty and working hard and making it. I tell them that I know I worked hard and changed my ways, but that I could not have done it without the help of my teacher and the mentors who guided me along the way.

The teachers admired my story and my hard work in college, and they hired me. I had landed a dream job. "You mean I get paid to help little youngsters go to school and get good grades?" I thought to myself, when I was invited to take the job by my new bosses.

I worked with young people whom schools had given up on, youngsters who had been to juvi, who were regularly suspended, who "gangbanged," and who did not show up to class. I connected with them by telling my story and by allowing them to tell me their story. I told the school administrators, "I will do the job but you've got to let me work with these kids at their level." The administrators agreed. Whenever the kids were not in school, I would go out and track them down. I hung out with them when they ditched class; they kicked it at the park, at the arcade, and in front of their apartment complex. The students were impressed by the fact that I was willing to help them out at their level, even if it meant hanging out with them while they were ditching school.

One day, rival gangs were preparing to start a riot at the school. A few of the boys, I had heard, had knives on them. I was stressed, "Do I tell the principal and have him call the police and have the police arrest the boys, and then later have the boys settle this on the street and possibly kill each other? Or do I have them come up with a more peaceful solution?" It was a risk, but I knew I had to respect the power and ideas of the youth in order for them to take responsibility. I brought a shot-caller from each of the gangs to my office.

"How can we solve this without having to bring in the police?" I asked.

"Let's throw down," one of them replied.

"Yea, let's duke it out," the other one responded.

"Impossible," I thought to myself. Then, out of nothingness, lacking a systematic solution, I blurted out, "O.K. Let's hold a boxing tournament, at the park, after school. Bring all the homies." The boys agreed. As they left my office, I began to regret my solution. "What am I gonna' do now?" I had four hours to prepare.

During lunch, the school was at peace. A riot did not break out. The teachers and administrators were impressed. "How did you do it, Victor?" an assistant principal asked.

"Um, I just talked to them and had them come up with their own solution," I responded.

"Wow! And what was their solution?" the assistant principal asked.

"Ah, they're going to have a meeting and talk it out without the school or police being involved," I replied.

"Will you be there?" he asked.

I exhaled a deep breath of stress, "Yes I will," I responded.

In preparation, I ran to my office and made some calls. I called two "older heads" from the two gangs who I knew would help me help the young people remain calm while the boxing matches were taking place. They agreed to show up. I arrived at the park early and setup a makeshift boxing ring. The youngsters arrived. Each side brought at least 20 homies. I took a deep breath. The older homies arrived. I asked them to help me regulate by being on each of the fighters' corners. They agreed. The first two boys put on the boxing gloves and the head-gear I had brought with me. They fought. One of them got a nose-bleed. We stopped the fight. At the end, without us telling them, they shook hands. Here were two kids who were ready to stab each other in the middle of the schoolyard, and now, they had settled their dispute. The sacrifices for this exchange, I felt, were not too big--a nose bleed, maybe an irate parent, maybe me losing my job— compared to what could have happened if the riot had broken out—arrests, negative news for the school, expulsions, injuries, and death.

I did not continue to host boxing tournaments for too much longer. Once the boys got a chance to learn how to resolve conflict without the use of regulated violence, I was able to convince them to have meetings, talk over the conflict, and participate in conflict resolution sessions. That year, we drastically reduced student violence at the school. Once I gained their trust and respect, I influenced the "at-risk" students to show up at school. I did so by giving them a point system for showing up to class and to my after-school tutoring program. I recruited college students to mentor then. Eventually, many of them became regular students at school again. They no longer needed to ditch school to feel accomplished; they felt self-worth and respect from an adult at the school, and this led many to work hard to do well in their classes.

16

12 Dozen Roses

To get a woman's heart,

a man must first use his own.

-Mike Dobbertin

Many of the students who had been excluded, suspended, and disciplined by the schools I eventually worked in, gained trust and respect for me. They came to me when they needed to share their problems and to ask for guidance. I helped them as much as I could. When I invested in these young people, I did not expect anything in return except that they do well in school and make healthier choices. Many of these youngsters returned the favor by making a firm choice to improve in school and avoid solving their problems with their attitudes. But these little sixth, seventh, and eighth graders would also personally pay me back in an incredible way.

I had a co-worker, a student-teacher, at one of the schools where I worked. She was a graduate student being trained to become a teacher. Her name was Rebeca Mireles. I interacted with her regularly because she taught some of the students I worked with. She was always concerned for some of the boys who were still involved in the gang. We talked about potential solutions. Rebeca was extremely smart and knew exactly what the students needed. She was charming with them and gave them respect. In turn, they respected her. Even though I thought that Rebeca was brilliant and beautiful, I gave her all the respect in the world, and kept my distance. I did not want her to think I was trying to make a move on her. I wanted Rebeca, and the rest of the school, to know that I was a real professional who could keep his attractions from interfering with his work.

However, the middle school students knew that Rebeca and I could be a perfect match for each other. We were like-minded, both of us adored working with students, and we were the same age and single. One day, Rebeca reccounts, a group of them went to Rebeca and told her, "Hey, Ms. Mireles, if you go out on a date with Mr. Rios, we'll wash your car for you. You know your car is really dirty? It's so dirty we wrote, 'wash me please,' on the window the other day."

Rebeca responded, "You guys are crazy. Did he put you up to this?"

One of them responded, "No, but we know he likes you." She ignored them and walked away.

Later that day, the kids came to me and said, "Ms. Mireles said she wants to go out on a date with you!"

"Oh, no," I thought to myself, "now I'm really going to get fired. I hope she doesn't think I put the kids up to this. I have to talk to her."

I approached Rebeca and told her, "Ms. Mireles, I am sorry for what the kids told you. I did not instruct them to tell you whatever it is they told you." She looked at me and smiled with her stunning-mesmerizing-enchanting smile. My heart pounded in my chest like the bass of a giant speaker at a rap concert.

She replied, "It's cool. Don't worry about it. I should probably take them up on the car wash."

I said, "Yea, I think your car really needs a wash. Um, do you, would you, do you think, um, maybe we can…"

She interrupted, "Hang out?"

"Yeah, hang out. Maybe do dinner sometime?" I asked.

"Sure," she replied. I felt like my heart was going to rip through my chest, I was so excited but I made sure to keep my cool, I slowly walked away with swagger. Rebeca and I went out on date. The kids washed her car.

Rebeca and I continued to date. We told each other that we thought we were good partners for each other because we had worked at making it in school and at becoming professionals. Choosing a partner who had demonstrated responsibility was important to both of us because we each knew that we wanted to one day marry someone who could provide for a family and teach his or her children the right morals, responsibilities, and values.

Two years after meeting Rebeca, I decided to ask her to marry me. I knew she was the right person for me because she helped me hold myself accountable to being a good person, to respecting her, and to delivering on my commitments. I loved Rebeca so much that I decided to sell the only investment I had at the time: a 1962 Chevrolet Impala. The Impala was my heart and joy. I would spend hours under the hood working on the carburetor, rebuilding the engine, and adjusting the gaps on the spark plugs. Those hours I spent under the hood helped me meditate, reflect, and become one with the car. It was a way for me to relieve stress. The Impala was cherry red with an all original, perfect condition, burgundy interior. It had glass pack mufflers, giving it one of the sweetest purrs a car enthusiast could ever hear. It was painful to sell my car, but I knew that I was doing it for the right reason. After selling the Impala, I walked into a jewelry store and purchased a diamond engagement ring.

On our last day of teaching, on a hot June afternoon, I arrived at Rebeca's classroom with twelve dozen long stemmed roses. I asked her co-workers to pull her out of class before I brought in the roses. Then I walked into the classroom and asked students to take a bunch of roses each and to hand them to Ms. Mireles when she walked back into the classroom. I hid under her desk with the ring in my hand. When she returned to class, the students rushed her with the twelve dozen roses. She began to cry. I gave her a moment to enjoy the students, then I leapt out from under her desk, got on my knees, and asked, "Rebeca, honey, will you marry me?" She was stunned. She grabbed my hand and nodded yes. I placed the ring on her hand. A year later, we were married.

17

The
Twins

Children are like wet cement,
whatever falls on them
makes an impression.
-Haim Ginott

Impossible was no longer a word in my vocabulary. By age 22 I had left the streets, graduated high school, completed a college degree, and landed my dream job. However, I still felt incomplete. I had been through so many obstacles in life that I felt I had an obligation to push myself even further, to achieve one more monumental success. I knew I had yet to reach my full potential. I was driven to acquire a graduate degree.

Rebeca had already been to UC Berkeley for her Master's Degree and Teaching Credential. She taught me what graduate school was all about. Being with someone who was living a positive life and accomplishing positive things made me realize that I could also accomplish these amazing feats. I told myself that if I could survive all the traumas that life had given me, I could survive graduate school. I decided to work towards acquiring the highest degree awarded in this country, the Ph.D., a doctoral degree. A few months later, I had been accepted to UC Berkeley. I went to orientation and started my first classes. If college was difficult, graduate school seemed nearly impossible. I had to read 3 books per week and at the end of the semester I had to turn in three thirty page papers. To top it all off I had to learn even more complicated words and theories than in college.

As if my school work was not complicated enough, a week after starting my intense Ph.D. program, Rebeca found out she was pregnant. When we went to the doctor's office, she told us, "Are you ready for a surprise? You not only have one baby in there: you are having twins!"

Rebeca and I had a long conversation. I knew that I was probably not going to finish my degree, and that I would have to leave the program in order to help support our new family.

Rebeca told me, "Don't worry, you can go to school, when the kids are born you can stay at home with them the three days that you're not at school. You can be the father that you have always wanted to be." Rebeca understood me and my dream and for that I will always be grateful. I have found that one of the most amazing blessings I have received in life has been to find a partner who is there to support me and have her own ambitions to succeed in life.

Rebeca told me she would support me as I continued going to school but she also said, "Don't get too comfortable. I hear that people take seven to ten years to get their Ph.D. at Berkeley. I want you to finish in five years. If you don't, you will have to leave school and support the family." I agreed. A few months later, our twins, Marina Quetzalli (Nina) and Miriana Mayahuel (Maya), were born.

Having babies was one of the most amazing experiences in my life, and I made sure to deliver on the promise I had made to myself when I was a little kid, "If you're going to have kids, you better be there for them." I put myself to work taking care of my little ones in the daytime, while Rebeca went to work teaching. At night, when Rebeca came home, I went to work, staying up through the night reading for class, and writing the 30 page papers required for each of my classes.

Meanwhile, some of my classmates thought that I was taking on too much raising twins and being in graduate school. One of them later told me that they made a bet one day. 'I bet you that the homeboy from Oakland won't make it past the first year of graduate school,' one of them told the rest of the group.

A professor said to me, "You are the kid from Cal State, the one that barely made it into college. I heard about you. I told them not to admit you. I wanted to get this student from Brown University and you got in instead." He nodded his head in disgust.

I knew I had a lot to prove to myself, to Rebeca, to this professor, to my classmates, and to my community. So, while the twins and the rest of the world slept, I was up reading, writing, and learning, usually through the night until five in the morning.

When the twins were awake, I hung out with them. I put them in cardboard boxes and pulled them around with a rope tied to the boxes; I saddled them up on our dog Sancho and pretended they were riding a horse; I took them to my classes and my meetings at UC Berkeley.

I had lots of fun raising my daughters. One day when the twins and I played in my mother's back yard, a chicken flew into the yard. I asked my mother who did the chicken belong to. She told me that it was a wild chicken that flew into everyone's back yard. The girls, two-and-a-half years old at the time, and I chased the chicken down and captured it. We took it to our house where it became our pet. For three years the chicken lived in our backyard and the twins fed it every morning.

It was also hard work raising the twins while I went to school. However, it was an opportunity for me to experience the joys of a childhood that I never had. Nina and Maya were angel babies. They taught me a lot, and they helped me learn what fatherhood was all about. I thank my babies for being there for me and for teaching me how to be a good parent. Becoming a parent is one of the most amazing gifts that nature can provide a human being. However, the timing has to be right. By the time Rebeca and I had children we had both already acquired college degrees. If we needed money to pay for the costs of having children we had the option of leaving graduate school and finding a good paying job. Luckily, Rebeca's teacher's income kept us afloat as the twins grew up and I worked on my Ph.D.

In order to graduate, I had to write a 200 page book known as a dissertation. The twins gave me the courage and strength to finish. I would have to put food on the table very soon, and the only way to do it was to finish my degree. In 2005, five years after starting my Ph.D. program, I became Dr. Rios. I received my first job offer as a professor at the University of San Francisco, one of the youngest ever hired there, age 26, a few months before my graduation.

18

Dr. Rios

The philosophers have only
interpreted the world, in various
ways; the point is to change it.
-Karl Marx

I became Dr. Rios to accomplish a mission: to learn
to be a good father, to redeem the death of my best
friend, to help my family, to empower my
community, and to help marginalized young people.
While I don't feel that I have done enough to make a
drastic change in this world, I believe that I have
done my part and that I continue to do so everyday.
Today, I am a professor of sociology at UC Santa
Barbara, where I teach students about the struggles
and obstacles that marginalized young people in our
country face. Sociology is the study of society, the
study of how and why people behave the way they do
and create groups, institutions, and organizations
that have a lasting impact on the world around us. I
lead mentoring programs, where we go out into the
community and help young people who have been
labeled "criminals" and "gang bangers."

Despite the fact that school wasn't for me, that the
many obstacles in my life made it nearly impossible
for me to make it; at one point, I decided to make
school for me. I decided to hold myself accountable
for my actions, to take advantage of the

opportunities that were presented to me, and to crack open the doors to success.

Recently, Rebeca and I added one more baby to the family. His name is Marco Ometeotl. Again, I am invigorated to continue to succeed and to raise my children in the right way, by helping others who have not been given opportunity, so that we can make this world a better place. I know that if I do my part, I will inspire others to do the same.

I know that if young people read my story, they might become inspired to lift themselves out of neglect and adversity. I know that if we all do our parts, young people, who, we think, will never make it, will return and tell us, "because of you, I became Dr. Johnson, Dr. Ramirez, Dr. Rios." I know that those young people who have gotten this far in this book have the power to believe in themselves and improve their lives. I know that they have the strength to become record breakers, to redeem themselves, and to accomplish the unbelievable. These same young people who have been labeled as bad, criminal, gang banging, or irreparable, can one day return to the stage of life to show of their degrees and successes and they too can receive a standing ovation. I believe that my struggles and crazy experiences made me the successful person that I am today. Even though my adversity forced me to tell myself that school was not for me, I eventually taught myself that education would be my only true salvation. I believe in the power of the youth, in the amazing ability that young people have to be resilient and survive even the most extreme adversities.

Every journey begins with a single step. Today is the day to make that move and show yourself and the world that anything is possible. If I, Victor Rios, could do it--if I could go through the stages of Poverty, Gangs and a Ph.D.--imagine what you can do?

Acknowledgments

I am deeply thankful to the communities of struggle where I was raised. My mother Raquel, brother J.T., brother Mike, and sister Rosa are all still part of my tight-knit family, despite the many adversities we faced. The homies who shared the streets with me and backed me up when I needed a home, protection, money, or affirmation, you know who you are, and I thank you with all my heart. I thank my teacher, Ms. Russ, and the many other adults who took the time and care to look out for my well-being and make it possible for me to believe in myself. I also want to thank the individuals who read this book and gave me feedback: Lisa Bass Bordofsky, Ismael Huerta, Consuelo Castillo Kickbusch, Jillian Mariani, Heather Tirado-Delgado, my "Casa de la Raza" students at UCSB, and the homies who attend our Casa de la Raza group. Andrew Huerta provided the art for the cover of this book. Richard Santana, from *Homeboy goes to Harvard,* first encouraged me to share my story with young people and helped me develop my presentation. I have made it this far thanks to the support and encouragement of my decade-long, companion-partner-best-friend-wife, Rebeca Mireles. My in-laws, Nadine, Enrique, Anita, Darrell, Sarita and Rona have taken me in as their own son and brother. My twin daughters, Maya and Marina, and son Marco have taught me how to be a good father while attempting to help and inspire young people. To all of you, I am deeply grateful.

Made in the USA
San Bernardino, CA
21 October 2013